MW01634504

ELTON JOHN

shall

ELTON JOHN

MICK ST. MICHAEL

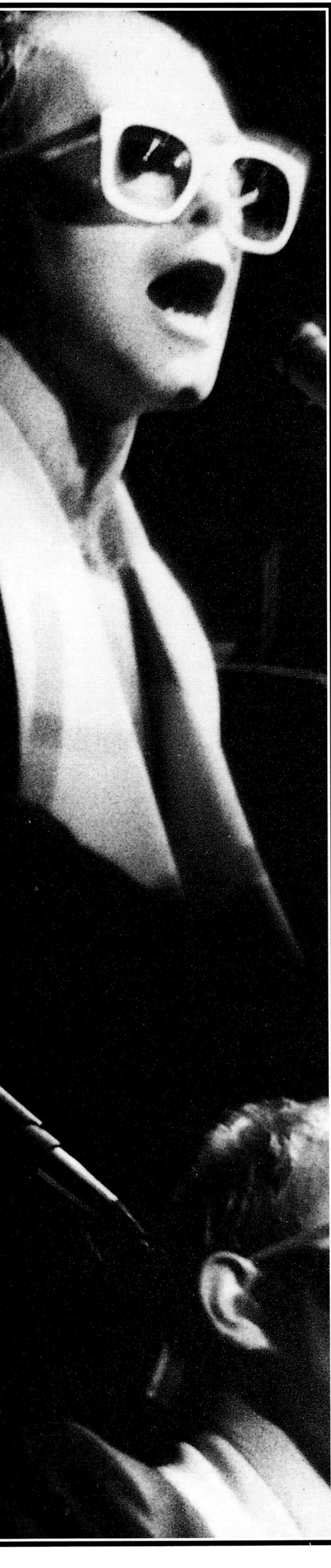

Contents

First published in 1994 by

Bison Books Ltd.
Kimbolton House
117A Fulham Road
London SW3 6RL

ISBN 1-85841-090-8

Printed in China

Page 1: Elton John in mid-song at the Rainbow Theater, London in May 1977.

Pages 2-3: A typically flamboyant Elton John, rehearsing for the Royal Variety Performance in October 1972.

Left: The many faces of Elton John – a composite image captured on his British tour in May 1976.

Introduction

If rock was born when Elvis swiveled his hips, the inheritors of Presley's mantle were the guitar heroes, posing, preening and plucking. Few pianists have emerged from behind their keyboards to become stars in their own right, and those who have – like Little Richard and Jerry Lee Lewis – have enjoyed the benefit of larger-than-life personalities, not to mention eccentric states of mind. No one who saw Reginald Kenneth Dwight as he took his first hesitant steps to fame would have put the pudgy youngster from Pinner, England, in that league; indeed, a charisma transplant would have been deemed necessary for him to play even a bit part in some other star's success story.

Yet, as Elton John, he stands at the very pinnacle of a rock world with which, superficially at least, he seemed to have precious little in common. A curious anomaly, the master of the personal, sensitive ballad hid behind his vast collection of exotic outfits – glitter waistcoats, feather-trimmed jumpsuits and the like – to acquire the showman image that found success in the United States. Even more curiously, the man who delivered those diaries-in-song was responsible for the music but not the words.

Elton John's meeting with Lincolnshire-born lyricist Bernie Taupin was certainly significant in bringing the two ingredients of words and music together. But at the time it seemed unlikely that the pair would rise higher than the level of Tin Pan Alley tunesmiths, patiently beavering away behind the scenes to provide Tom Jones and the like with their next smash hit. The likelihood of Reg Dwight himself being in the spotlight was far-fetched to say the least. It is a curious turn of events which he continues to find amusing. 'I'm a tubby little singer,' he once said, 'and I can't understand why people scream for me. There must be a reason, but God knows what it is . . .'

Left: Elton in his most familiar guise: seated at the piano, wearing a garish stage costume – and delighting his audience in the process.

Right: Elton dressed in untypically sober garb. However, his trademark spectacles, unorthodox headgear and flashy jewelry are still very much in evidence.

CHAPTER ONE
Hello Yellow Brick Road

The infant Reginald Kenneth Dwight did *his* first screaming at half past midnight on 25 March 1947 in Pinner, Middlesex, a nondescript outer suburb of London. His father Stanley, then a Royal Air Force officer, had enjoyed an earlier career as a professional trumpeter, so from an early age there was music in the family. As with so many children, piano lessons were instigated but, unlike the majority, young Reg took to the keyboard like a duck to water. His earliest idols were Charlie Kunz and Winifred Atwell . . . until, that is, his mother Sheila brought home a couple of new 'pop' records that were to change the nine-year-old's life. 'They were Elvis's "Heartbreak Hotel" and Bill Haley's "ABC Boogie." They were the first big influences in my life. I loved banging away at those two numbers on piano.'

Thirsting for knowledge, the youngster happened upon a magazine article on Elvis while waiting in the local barber's for a trim. 'The way he performed seemed incredible,' Elton confessed later. 'Then I saved my pocket money and bought Little Richard's "She's Got It" and "The Girl Can't Help It." '

It is interesting in retrospect to see how quickly the budding pianist gravitated toward a suitable role model, although the opinion of Mrs Dwight was somewhat different! Her reluctance to allow the songs of 'Little Richard' Penniman to be played in the Dwight domicile only increased Reg's determination. 'My aim was to be a pop star or at least something to do with the business,' he later recalled, adding with a touch of realism, 'even if it was only selling records in a shop.'

His father was not quite so keen, and did little to encourage his son's daydreaming. But the Dwights' divorce removed him from the scene, and young Reg inevitably enjoyed rather more freedom to do as he pleased. Not that classical exercises were totally

Opposite page: A six-year-old Reg Dwight (far left) acts as a page boy at the wedding of his soccer-star cousin, Roy Dwight.

This page: To his parents' dismay, the young Reg Dwight was heavily influenced by some of the great legends of rock and roll, including: *left*, Bill Haley and the Comets; *below left*, 'Little Richard' Penniman; and *below*, Jerry Lee Lewis.

Far left: Elton modeled much of his extrovert stage act on that of a childhood idol, Little Richard. However, by 1974 he had developed his own brand of inimitable style.

Left: Elvis Presley, pictured here in 1956. His recording of 'Heartbreak Hotel' would change the course of Reg Dwight's life.

neglected: the lad was conscientious, and shortly after his first public appearance at the age of 12 at a local festival of music, he was offered a scholarship to London's prestigious Royal Academy of Music. This did not mean a total disruption of his regular life – the lessons, which went on for some five years, were on Saturday mornings – but it helped to add some much-needed confidence to his keyboard abilities. Reg had also passed his 11-Plus exam to qualify for Pinner County Grammar School, entering in 1958.

The next step was a little divergence from the straight-and-narrow classical route: playing pop music! His first group, formed with Stuart Brown, a young guitarist friend of his cousin, was christened the Corvettes after a popular brand of aftershave. Initially unimpressed by the overweight Master Dwight, Brown relented when the lad demonstrated his musical prowess – including an impressive Jerry Lee Lewis impersonation. Local boy-scout huts provided the venues for these adolescent ventures, although the group had no proper amplification system and it inevitably fell through after a few months.

Reg's next venture was a solo one. Now approaching school-leaving age, he persuaded a local hotelier at the Northwood Hills Hotel to give him a trial entertaining his clientele on Fridays, Saturdays and Sundays. The musical fare was hardly Jerry Lee Lewis – Jim Reeves-style country ballads went down particularly well with the good people of Pinner – but there *was* money in it. 'They paid a small wage and let me take a box round,' he recalls. 'The customers were kind, and soon I had enough to buy an electric piano.' A reunion with Stuart Brown, now also somewhat better equipped than in the Corvettes' days, followed, and the road to stardom beckoned.

Perhaps the destination seemed a little nearer than it really was, for an intrepid Reg left Pinner County Grammar School some weeks before taking his examinations. There was already a star in the family – elder cousin Roy Dwight, the Nottingham Forest soccer player who became famous for breaking his leg in the 1959 FA Cup Final against Luton – and he had heard of an opening in the music business. It is doubtful that this warranted the boy quitting school without qualifica-

tions, especially as the job in publishing at Mills Music involved little more than being an errand boy and tea-maker, but Reg needed no second bidding; the negligible weekly wages were incidental.

Having put one foot firmly on the first rung of the ladder to a career in music, Reg Dwight was quick to swing the other one up too. In this case, it was membership of Bluesology, the semiprofessional band he formed with Stuart, named after a record by jazz guitarist Django Reinhardt. They successfully auditioned one Saturday morning at the Kilburn State movie theater for the Roy Tempest agency, which booked them to back visiting American soul and rhythm-and-blues stars of the caliber of Wilson Pickett, Major Lance, the Drifters, Patti LaBelle and the Bluebelles, Doris Troy and many others. Alongside Reg and Stuart, Bluesology's first line-up featured bassist Geoff Dyson and drummer Mick Inkpen.

Although Stuart Brown was nominally lead vocalist, Reg had pushed his way to the microphone on a number of occasions (including for two self-penned singles, 'Come Back Baby' and 'Mr Frantic,' released in July 1965 and February 1966), only to find that his singing was not widely appreciated. Indeed, Bluesology took on a permanent vocalist in 1967 in the shape of Long John Baldry, a relatively experienced blues singer. It was something of a step-up in status, though the increased fees had to be shared nine ways when a brass section was grafted onto the original line-up.

The band's decision to throw in its lot with Baldry seemed to be the right one when he scored a surprise No. 1 hit single with the mighty but unquestionably middle-of-the-road 'Let The Heartaches Begin.' These were exciting times, but Reg was rapidly becoming disenchanted with the round of nightclubs and middle-aged audiences to whom he was being asked to play.

Left: A dynamic combination: Bernie Taupin and Reg Dwight, whose fortuitous introduction to each other by Liberty Records would result in one of the greatest musical partnerships in the history of rock music.

Right: Long John Baldry, the lead singer with Reg's early band, Bluesology, and the inspiration for Reg's new surname.

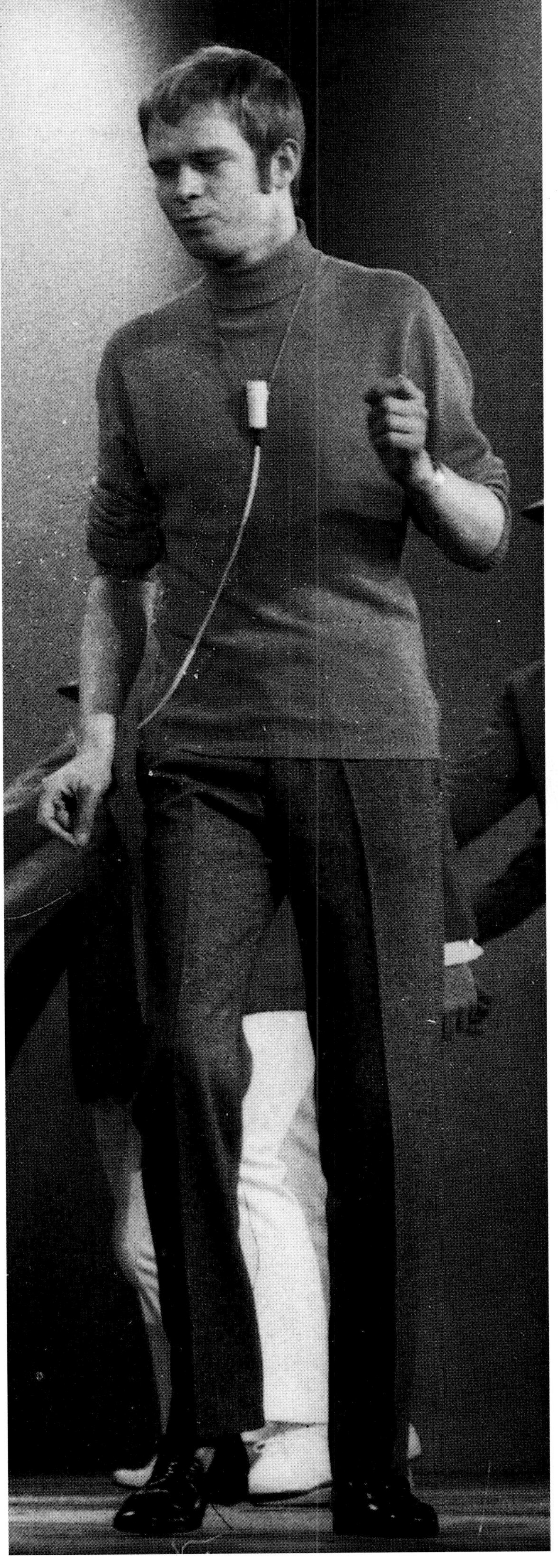

This was not what Reg had left Mills Music for.

Bluesology's own records were universal failures (a third, 'Since I Met You Baby' came out in 1967), and indeed Reg's first attempt to break away – an audition at Liberty Records, a US label in the process of setting up a London office – had proved equally unsuccessful. (Legend has it that he sang five consecutive Jim Reeves numbers, since these were the only ones whose words he could be guaranteed to remember!) Liberty Records did, however, suggest that he join forces with a lyricist whose response to the same music-press advertisement which Reg had answered had initially been retrieved from the trash can and posted by his mother! His name was Bernie Taupin.

Reg's new opposite number, at 18 three years younger than him, had already left school and gone through a number of jobs, including chicken farming and print operating for a local newspaper. Once introduced, they linked up with Gralto Music, a firm of song publishers which had been successful with the Hollies. However, it was not long before Dick James, the man who had published Lennon and McCartney's hit songs, took them under his wing. The weekly payments were enough for Reg to throw in his Bluesology gig and turn full-time professional songwriter (although he played occasional gigs with the Bread and Beer Band, a group of session musicians). He took no independent legal advice on the contract that he and Bernie were signing, a fact that would lead to problems in the future. 'In all good faith, I just signed it,' he said later. 'I was very green behind the ears . . .'

Dick James had also signed him as an artist, and so it was that he came to record his first single. 'I've Been Loving You' was scarcely an earth-shattering title, but Reg Dwight was even more mundane a name to have underneath it on the label of a seven-inch single. A new name was called for – and *quickly*. Combining the first names of saxophonist Elton Dean and Long John Baldry resulted in 'Elton John,' much as Harry Webb had settled on 'Cliff Richard' a decade before. 'I'd had a terrible inferiority complex as Reg Dwight,' Elton later confessed, 'and the name change helped me get out of it.' Not that he found this choice totally satisfactory, however. 'Later I thought about changing it again, but no one could come up with anything better.' Later still, Reg Dwight would legally change his name to Elton Hercules John.

CHAPTER TWO
The Troubadour and the Trio

If his name was not yet up in lights, the newly-christened Elton John was winning attention on several fronts. He and Bernie got a song, 'I Can't Go On Living Without You,' into the last six entries of the Eurovision Song Contest; while unsuccessful, it would later be recorded by Cilla Black. (The winning entry, 'Boom Bang-A-Bang,' won Lulu the contest.) Urbane actor Edward Woodward cut the duo's composition 'The Tide Will Turn For Rebecca,' while a number of singers picked up on their 'Skyline Pigeon' without anyone actually having a hit with it.

The next Elton John release, January 1969's 'Lady Samantha,' on the Philips label, was a 'turntable hit,' receiving more airplay than sales, but was later picked up and covered by American group Three Dog Night. Interestingly, the session drummer on this release and on Elton's first album was Roger Pope, who would join his band in the mid-1970s. The singer betrayed a certain lack of confidence, however, in the month of the record's release by hedging his bets and auditioning unsuccessfully for a new, progressive rock group being formed by guitarist Robert Fripp; this would later emerge as King Crimson.

Producer Steve Brown continued at the helm for an unspectacular first album, *Empty Sky*, on Dick James' new DJM label, before bowing out; as a last act, he recommended that Elton link up with arranger Paul Buckmaster to record his next album. Buckmaster had just worked on the debut hit for another singer-songwriter, David Bowie, with producer Gus Dudgeon – and while the album *Elton John* which resulted did not contain a 'Space Oddity,' it did include three *bona fide* future classics in 'Take Me To The Pilot,' 'Border Song' (later to be be recorded by no less a personality than soul doyenne Aretha Franklin), and the opening 'Your Song.' In addition, though not a hit, Elton played on one

Far left: The unimaginatively-named Elton John Group, seen here in 1972 in the company of Legs Larry Smith (wearing the hat).

Left: From left to right, drummer Nigel Olsson, bassist Dee Murray, Elton, and guitarist Davey Johnstone, pictured in 1972, the year of *Honky Château.*

Left: In 1972 rising star Elton John still dressed relatively conservatively. However, the shoes on prominent display are an early indication of things to come.

Right: A crowd of enthusiastic fans clamors to have Elton autograph their copies of the phenomenally successful *Don't Shoot Me, I'm Only the Piano Player*, released in January 1973.

of the Hollies' releases – 'He Ain't Heavy . . . He's My Brother' – recorded at London's legendary Abbey Road studios.

Having cut four hits with different artists, from Bowie to the Bonzo Dog Band, Gus Dudgeon had been looking for 'one artist who wrote a lot of great songs. Elton and his manager played me this demo tape and I thought, "My God, there's so much good material . . ." It was exactly what I wanted.' The partnership would last through to 1976. The album took just a week to record, recalls Dudgeon. 'Even as we were making it we knew it was special. What we wondered was whether anybody else would recognize it as being anything at all . . . '

As well as having a producer, Elton now had a band of sorts: a rhythm section consisting of drummer Nigel Olsson (who had previously been with Plastic Penny) and bassist Dee Murray, who had played together in the Spencer Davis Group. Olsson had been brought up in Sunderland in the north of England and could play numerous other nonpercussion instruments, while Murray (real name David Murray Oates), who was one year older than Elton, was born in Kent and brought up in London. Although Caleb Quaye (the DJM sound engineer who helped Elton to get his break) did the honors in the studio, there was no guitarist in the stage line-up, a fact that made it pretty obligatory for Elton to ham it up and act his flamboyant best.

The line-up made its recording debut on *Elton John*, released in April 1970. On the evidence of the album, Uni Records claimed the group for America; as the label that had signed Neil Diamond, it clearly recognized a singer-songwriter of promise.

In the wake of this signing, the trio were sent out to the United States for a series of showcase gigs which started with a week at Los Angeles' prestigious Troubadour Club which was celebrating its twentieth anniversary in a blaze of media attention. From the outset, when Leon Russell turned up to take his seat in the front row, it was obvious that there was a buzz about town for this unknown Englishman in his yellow overalls, Donald Duck bib and aluminum boots. Graham Nash, the Beach Boys, Quincy Jones, Gordon Lightfoot and others joined the throng as the residency progressed, and the press coverage was nothing short of sensational. *Los Angeles Times* critic Robert Hilburn's reaction was typical. 'Rejoice,' he said, 'Rock, which has been going through a rather uneventful period lately, has a new star!'

After returning briefly to Britain at the end of his three-week tour, Elton soon found the demand for more American appearances overwhelming. By November 1970 *Elton John* had sold 250,000 copies in its ascent to the dizzy heights of No. 4, while the soon-to-be-released *Tumbleweed Connection* would do nearly as well. The coming year, 1971, would bring a surfeit of record releases: apart from his third and fourth albums, *Tumbleweed Connection* and *Madman Across The Water*, Elton had scored the film *Friends* with Paul Buckmaster, while a live radio-show broadcast in the United States by New York's WPLJ-FM radio was released as *17.11.70* (or *11.17.70*, depending on which side of the Atlantic it was sold) and reached No. 20 in Britain and 11 in the States without the aid of a hit single.

From being a total unknown, Elton John had released five albums in four years and had become an international star.

Britain had finally caught on to the Elton John phenomenon, and 'Your Song' was lifted into chart contention in early 1971; *Elton John* itself reached No. 11. Indeed, the rewards had already proved enough for Elton to buy a bungalow on an exclusive private estate in Wentworth which boasted Rod Stewart (an old friend) and Donovan as neighbours. *Tumbleweed Connection* added to those rewards, becoming his first British Top 10 album. Its No. 6 position was beaten by one place in the *Billboard* listings, Britain and America in total accord as to the album's excellence. The bulk of this phenomenal success was down to the quality of the songwriting.

However, new material was already on the way from the prolific duo, in the shape of two singles: 'Levon,' which reached No. 24 in the States, and 'Tiny Dancer,' No. 41. Both were taken from the forthcoming *Madman Across The Water* album – a relative failure in Britain, where it peaked one place short of the all-important Top 40, but which was pushed to No. 8 stateside by Elton's faithful American following. Appropriately enough, as with *Tumbleweed Connection*, the album reflected Bernie Taupin's fascination with life on the more glamorous side of the Atlantic.

The *Billboard* chart was (and is) compiled on the strength of a combination of airplay and sales, so Elton's radio-friendliness was clearly another contributing factor to his success. Furthermore, *Madman Across The Water*, its lyrics faithfully rendered in copperplate in the enclosed libretto, fitted fairly and squarely within the popular confessional singer-songwriter school headed by the likes of Carole King and James Taylor. Interestingly, the song 'Tiny Dancer' was dedicated 'with love to Maxine': Elton had not encouraged speculation as to his sexuality, but lines about 'laying down in sheets of linen' suggested nothing out of the ordinary. Then you recalled that Bernie (the only other person pictured in the booklet) wrote the words and that Maxine was his American wife. Not for the last time, it seemed that Elton was a blank canvas upon which his partner's thoughts could be expressed.

The band expanded to a four-piece in early 1972, with the addition of ex-Magna Carta man Davey Johnstone, a lanky Scot with flowing blond hair who doubled on lute, sitar, mandolin and banjo. Johnstone increased the potential for flat-out rock'n'roll and, said Elton, 'took pressure off the rest of us . . . ,' adding 'it was either change completely or split.' He had first appeared as one of several featured guitarists on *Madman Across The Water*, but made his debut as a full band member on *Honky Château*, named after the Château d'Herouville just outside Paris where the album was recorded in spring 1972. It took just three weeks to record the album, which included Elton's

Far left: By 1973 – the year of *Goodbye Yellow Brick Road* – Elton was on a roll. His American tour set new records – both for attendance and for outrageousness.

Left: Proudly displaying Elton's gold disk for 'Rocket Man' in September 1972 are, from left to right, Bernie Taupin, Elton and Dick James, whose DJM label had released the hit single.

second breakthrough single to follow 'Your Song' into the all-time classics listings.

'Rocket Man' captured the public imagination in rather the same way that Bowie's 'Space Oddity' had done, and eclipsed 'Your Song' as Elton's most successful British single. It soared to No. 2 (as did the album), only T Rex's 'Metal Guru' keeping it from the top spot. Surprisingly, it only reached No. 6 in America; perhaps the novelty of space flight was not quite as captivating there.

Despite the success of both single and album – which topped the US chart – Elton continued on the tour/album treadmill. Having found the château an easy place in which to work ('you were in the middle of nowhere,' he said, 'so you couldn't yield to temptation . . . you stayed put and did what you had to do'), Elton returned there in June 1972 and, despite a case of glandular fever, decided that he would 'have it all over with' before his holiday, booked for the following month. Yet on unpacking his bags he found that he only had one complete song, and had to persuade Bernie Taupin to send him the remaining lyrics from America. The result was the amazingly successful *Don't Shoot Me, I'm Only The Piano Player*, released just eight months after its predecessor, in January 1973.

Given the speed with which the album was put together, it was reassuring that the two singles from *Don't Shoot Me . . .* hit the upper-chart echelons in record time. 'Crocodile Rock' was a 1950s pastiche, almost a throwaway song, but a catchy one, that paid musical homage to Neil Sedaka (who, interestingly, would be the first signing to Elton's Rocket Records label later in the decade). America fittingly took the song to its heart, giving Elton his first No. 1 single there. Then came 'Daniel,' another reflective ballad in time-honored style, with enigmatic Taupin lyrics. Inspired by a *Newsweek* story about a Vietnam hero who quit his hometown in an effort to forget his war exploits, it was written and recorded in a day and made No. 2 in the United States. Both singles prospered in the British charts, at Nos. 5 and 4 respectively, while the album itself was Elton's first to top both British and American charts – a feat achieved within three weeks of its release. DJM had refused to release 'Daniel' as a single, considering it not only uncommercial but too different to its predecessor to succeed, and Elton therefore had to pay for the advertising himself. Needless to say he had the last laugh.

Elton was turning into a hit machine, and certainly was not going to let the grass grow under his feet. Yet a château hat trick of hits proved impossible since he had planned to record his next album in February 1973. Finding his favored French studio closed, he switched location to Jamaica, where he found the conditions equally conducive to creativity. Having finished *Don't Shoot Me . . .* with two spare songs in hand, another 20 were added to his repertoire in a matter of days. Sadly, however, despite Gus Dudgeon's earlier reconnaissance trip, the recording facilities in Jamaica left something to be desired, and when the grand piano Elton

Right: Elton John pictured in 1975, guesting as a BBC Radio One disk jockey for a day.

Far right: At 29 years of age, Elton had made it. Having bought an English mansion at Virginia Water, Surrey, he proceeded to fill it with all manner of unusual obejcts. 'I just collect things. It drives my mum mad,' joked Elton.

wanted could not be obtained, it proved the final straw: all 22 songs were promptly stowed in his hand luggage and taken back to France. Conceived in Jamaica and recorded at the château, *Goodbye Yellow Brick Road* would prove Elton's masterpiece to date.

Surprisingly, the album was not released on his own Rocket Records label (named after his 'Rocket Man' hit and launched with characteristic fanfare in May 1973); he would remain on DJM for half-a-dozen albums yet. Rocket Records would never prove a spectacular success, but made initial waves when its signing, Kiki Dee, a British singer who had always meant more in the States than at home, scored a series of hits including 'Amoureuse' and 'I've Got The Music In Me.' In addition, Neil Sedaka's career was relaunched with Rocket Records, while Cliff Richard was signed for the United States and made a long-awaited commercial impact with 'Devil Woman.' Of the lesser-known names, future Eurythmic Dave Stewart was briefly aboard the Rocket train as a member of Longdancer. Based in Wardour Street in London's Soho, the record company's directors were Elton, Bernie, Gus Dudgeon, Steve Brown and manager John Reid, who had exerted quite an influence on Elton's life and career since leaving EMI Records in 1971 to take charge of his business affairs.

Reid, a quiet Scot who had quickly risen through the ranks at EMI Records to become the London label manager of Tamla-Motown Records, initially managed Elton's business affairs on DJM's behalf. In 1973 he took sole charge, and would continue in this capacity over the next 20 years, ruling with a firm hand and only occasionally taking on other clients (Queen was briefly under his umbrella). It is doubtful if Elton could have weathered the music-business and media storms which he would encounter in the coming decades as successfully without Reid at his side.

Elton was clearly not going to take time out to play the record-company boss. His American tour of the summer of 1973, during which the touring party was flown across the States in a specially-painted jet airliner (complete with piano), smashed attendance records at almost every port of call. Longstanding house records, set as far back as Elvis Presley's days, were rewritten. The show, too, was extravagance itself, hitting a high point at the Hollywood Bowl on 7 September. Introduced to the 16,000-strong audience by porn queen Linda Lovelace as 'the Queen of England,' Elton descended a film-set staircase to camp it up among five differently-coloured grand pianos, the lids of which spelled E-L-T-O-N.

Goodbye Yellow Brick Road was a double album's worth of songs that ranged from the sublime to the

simply awful – among the latter 'Dirty Little Girl' and 'Jamaica Jerkoff,' a track that Elton later admitted 'makes me cringe.' But for every one of these there was also a classic. The mock aggression of 'Saturday Night's Alright For Fighting' was scarcely standard singer-songwriter fare, but was just one extreme of a highly varied collection. The title track, for example (also a major hit), mixed autobiography with the *Wizard of Oz*; while the opening blast of 'Funeral For A Friend' (featuring David Hentschel's howling synthesizer) and the rattling 'Love Lies Bleeding,' in which the lyrics seemed totally at odds with the music, were all carried off with perhaps Elton's ultimate show of recorded bravado.

'Grey Seal' was another rocker from the album, this time resurrected and rerecorded from the B-side of 1970's 'Rock And Roll Madonna.' But the track which critics and fans alike alighted on was 'Candle In The Wind,' yet another classic piano ballad, this time dedicated to Marilyn Monroe from a young fan. In America the single was flipped to reveal 'Bennie And The Jets,' a solid but perhaps unspectacular piece of white rhythm-and-blues, which staggered everyone by shooting to the top spot. It also reached No. 15 in the black-dominated R & B chart, sowing the seeds of further soulful offerings to come.

Returning to home turf, five seasonal sellout dates at London's Hammersmith Odeon, following hard on the heels of a Bryan Forbes TV documentary, ended the year in style. Less memorably, Elton also unleashed a Christmas single on the world: 'Step Into Christmas,' backed by 'Ho! Ho! Ho! (Who'd Be A Turkey At Christmas?)'. The year had also seen the band expand to accommodate percussionist Ray Cooper, who had previously worked with session supergroup Blue Mink, but had played on every one of Elton's albums since the first and was thus able to step out on stage at Liverpool without having rehearsed previously. The extrovert Cooper, who came from a jazz background, would enjoy a long professional relationship with Elton.

However, something had to give in this tireless merry-go-round of recording and touring. The next album – *Caribou*, recorded at the Denver, Colorado ranch of Chicago producer James William Guercio – was lackluster. Squeezed in between tour dates, the album was as uncharacteristically lacking in memorable melodies as *Goodbye Yellow Brick Road* had been an embarrassment of riches. 'Solar Prestige A Gammon,' a song built around a Taupin nonsense lyric, summed up the throwaway feel. No one was surprised when a British tour scheduled for April and May 1974 was canceled: the Rocket Man had run out of fuel.

Far left: By 1974 Elton's continuing success was assured. However, the grueling combination of album production and touring, into which Elton always put so much effort, was beginning to take its toll.

Left: Elton was always willing to diversify, and in February 1975 clearly relished his disguise for Cher's comedy show on US television.

Wisely, Elton took a break to recharge his batteries – and the difference was apparent when he returned to the States with his band, crossing in style on the luxury liner SS *France* and rehearsing his new material *en route*. America was clearly where his future shone brightest: MCA had renewed his contract at an estimated cost of $8,000,000; *Caribou* had sold well despite its shortcomings, while the outstanding track 'Don't Let The Sun Go Down On Me,' had become a million-seller, reaching the US No. 2 spot. (Amazingly, Elton had originally considered his performance of the song 'the worst vocal of all time' and did not want it included.) When tickets for an October run of three shows in Los Angeles sold out literally in minutes, a fourth had to be added, underlining Elton's continuing stateside popularity. Even a track like 'The Bitch Is Back,' by his own standards a substandard rewrite of 'Saturday Night's Alright For Fighting,' reached No. 4, while Elton's singles were drifting toward the high teens in the charts at home.

It was in America, too, that Elton formed an unusual artistic alliance with one of the most famous expatriate British musicians the country has ever played host to – John Lennon. The ex-Beatle invited Elton to guest on his album *Walls And Bridges*, adding piano to 'Surprise Surprise,' and the US No. 1 single 'Whatever Gets You Thru The Night.' Anxious to return the compliment, Elton persuaded Lennon to join him at Caribou for the next album's sessions, with the promise that they would be cutting an old song of his.

The result was 'Lucy In The Sky With Diamonds,' the allegedly drug-inspired classic from *Sgt Pepper*, and a Beatles number few had previously dared cover. 'John works the way I do in the studio,' explained Elton. 'We just had a laugh and I really have a very strong affection for him.'

That was to become apparent when Lennon was persuaded to make a guest appearance with Elton and his band at New York's Madison Square Garden – in effect, an adoptive hometown gig for Lennon. Fittingly, the date coincided with Thanksgiving, and a festive feeling was in the air. Two songs were obvious choices: Lennon's No. 1 'Whatever Gets You Thru The Night,' with John on lead vocals, and 'Lucy In The Sky With Diamonds,' (shortly to become Elton's third US chart-topper), with both men harmonizing on the chorus. But there was a difference of opinion on a third song, as Elton recalls. 'I suggested "Imagine." He replied "Oh no! *Boring*. I've done it before. Let's do a rock'n'roll song." So I thought of "I Saw Her Standing There" – first track on the first Beatles album.' The track was a Paul McCartney composition, and the bass player had originally sung lead. Perhaps surprisingly, Lennon went for the idea, and so it was that they finished with this number – so successfully that Elton later played the song again in London without superstar assistance.

There was a fascinating sequel to this concert: Lennon had been separated from his wife Yoko Ono, and had been enjoying what he later called his 'lost weekend' period of booze, drugs and debauchery. Yoko attended the concert, and encountered him backstage – an event, they later revealed, that brought them back together again. Having resolved their differences, the Lennons retired to domestic seclusion to raise a son, Sean. Sadly, the Madison Square Garden gig would turn out to be John's last public performance before his assassination in December 1980.

The year 1974 ended with a series of Christmas shows in London which would become a traditional event. The amazing sequence of album releases was maintained, albeit with *Elton John's Greatest Hits*, which was MCA's fastest-selling American release of all time and, indeed, the first-ever singles collection to top the US charts.

Elton had been diversifying on the quiet, making his debut in films with a cameo appearance in his friend Marc Bolan's *Born To Boogie*, directed by another

Right: The Pinball Wizard – alias Elton John – whose gigantic boots became legendary in their own right. The Who's rock opera *Tommy* would develop something of a cult following.

Left: Elton attends the *Tommy* premiere in March 1975.

Below: Elton and occasional doubles partner, tennis star Billie Jean King, for whom he wrote the song 'Philadelphia Freedom.'

ex-Beatle, Ringo Starr (for whom Elton and Bernie later wrote a song, 'Snookeroo'). The acting experience clearly whetted his appetite, for his next big-screen break was somewhat more substantial. The film was Ken Russell's movie version of The Who's rock opera *Tommy*, released in 1975. Elton played the Pinball Wizard in a pair of typically overstated platform-heeled boots.

The second Caribou recording sessions had produced not only 'Lucy In The Sky With Diamonds' but an autobiography-in-song, entitled *Captain Fantastic And The Brown Dirt Cowboy*, which chronicled the earliest days of the Elton John/Bernie Taupin relationship. The album's elaborate packaging included a poster of the cover design by *Butterfly Ball* creator Alan Aldridge, a scrapbook and a lyrics book. *Captain Fantastic* became the first album ever to enter the American charts at the very top – not even the Beatles had managed *that*. But in Britain, where DJM decided to price it as a double album, much to Elton's annoyance, it was held off the top spot by *The Best Of The Stylistics* – an ironic choice, since the spring of that year had seen Elton venture once more into African-American music. 'Philadelphia Freedom' was the result of sessions held with Thom Bell, the producer of successful vocal acts like the Detroit Spinners. A three-track EP, it topped the US chart and became Elton's second R & B chart entry there. In Britain the lead track 'Philadelphia Freedom' – written for Elton's friend, tennis player Billie Jean King and her team the Freedoms – reached No. 12.

Captain Fantastic's autobiographical nature made it yet more fascinating for the critics: the track that caused the most comment was 'Someone Saved My Life Tonight,' the story of a suicide attempt that turned out to be true. It told the tale of when Elton broke off his engagement to Linda Woodrow, a girl with whom he had lived in Islington, North London, with Bernie Taupin as lodger, at the time when they were working toward their breakthrough.

The release of the album saw the departure of Nigel Olsson and Dee Murray, stalwarts of the Elton John Band since 1970; they were replaced by drummer Roger Pope, and American bass player Kenny Passarelli, who had previously played with Eagles guitarist Joe Walsh in Barnstorm. Also around at this time were American-born second keyboardist James Newton-Howard, plus the ubiquitous Caleb Quaye. It was the end of an era . . . and the beginning of another.

CHAPTER THREE
Rocket to the Top

Above: In 1975 Elton was delighted to receive the accolade of a star on Hollywood's Walk of Fame.

Right: The mid- to late 1970s were Elton's prime years; by the 1980s both his musical and his sartorial approach had become more subdued.

The summer of 1975 saw Elton and his now largely American band make headlines stateside. At the Oakland Coliseum in June he jammed with the Doobie Brothers and the Eagles on 'Listen To The Music' and Chuck Berry's 'Carol,' celebrating the fifth anniversary of his US stage debut two months later by playing two fund-raising gigs at the LA Troubadour for the Jules Stein Eye Institute of UCLA. A British gig at Wembley Arena for 72,000, with the Beach Boys and the Eagles, saw Steely Dan guitarist Jeff 'Skunk' Baxter sitting in. It seemed Elton could do no wrong, hitting the top again in November with a new single, 'Island Girl' and an album, *Rock Of The Westies*. He became godfather to John and Yoko Lennon's son Sean, and received a star on Hollywood's Walk of Fame on 21 November, declared 'Elton John Day' in his honor. And as if all that was not enough, he ended the year by becoming the first artist since the Beatles back in 1966 to play Los Angeles' Dodger Stadium. Ever the extrovert, Elton had a Dodgers uniform made up, which won the crowd over even quicker than he had expected. Indeed, he had ensured the fervent support of a fraction of the crowd by flying in the entire Rocket Records office staff and their families in a chartered jet, all this being filmed for a TV spectacular. This period was arguably the peak of his showmanship, but the music was going through an uncertain patch.

Rock Of The Westies (a diabolical pun on 'West of the Rockies') was the second Elton John album to debut at the top of *Billboard*'s chart. In many respects it was *Caribou* all over again – a less than convincing collection of songs. Personnel changes could, of course, be cited as being responsible, but the British public was clearly less impressed than ever. 'Grow Some Funk of Your Own' became Elton's first single not to chart at home, though a rerecorded version of 'Pinball Wizard' evoked positive memories of his *Tommy* appearance and reached No. 7 in April 1976. The previous month had seen Elton's Hollywood star equaled by his appearance at Madame Tussaud's in London. He was the first pop star since the Beatles to be so honored, the conservative staff of the waxworks collection conceding that he was one musical hero unlikely to fade away.

In America Elton was nominated 'Worst Dresser,' while the paparazzi caught him leaving a central London movie theater with his friend Princess

Right: In 1976 Elton was honored to join the small but distinguished band of celebrities whose likenesses are displayed at Madame Tussaud's in London, England. Elton's waxwork was unique, in that it was the first talking model ever created.

Far right: Kiki Dee and Elton were a chart-topping partnership in 1976 with their song 'Don't Go Breaking My Heart.' In 1993 they would be reunited to sing 'True Love.'

Margaret, having been to see *The Sunshine Boys*. However, 1976 was also the year in which Elton gave the first overt clues as to his complex sexuality, in a *Rolling Stone* interview. 'There's nothing wrong with going to bed with someone of your own sex,' he bravely admitted. Surprisingly, there was little backlash from his fans in Britain, although things would be different a decade on, when a national newspaper took it upon itself to smear his name. In the United States, however, Elton believed 'it had a chilling effect on people. They didn't really want to know, and were offended.'

Elton now owed Dick James just one more album, which would be a live selection; the resulting *Here And There*, recorded in London and New York, was a trans-atlantic Top 10 entry. Although DJM retained the rights to a future *Greatest Hits* album, all Elton's future releases would now be on Rocket Records, 'home' of band members past and present Nigel Olsson and Davey Johnstone. Dee Murray meanwhile was touring the States (where he now lived), first with Procul Harum and then with Alice Cooper.

Real success, however, was left to the boss to achieve, and this he did with the assistance of 'Don't Go Breaking My Heart,' a duet performed with Kiki Dee. The song (written by Elton and Bernie under the pseudonyms of Ann Orson and Carte Blanche) would be memorably reprised twice on future occasions: firstly on *The Muppet Show*, with Miss Piggy taking Dee's place, and again in 1985 on the global stage that took Live Aid to an audience of 1.5 billion people. It was no

surprise that the song topped the charts in the United States, but it was pleasing that it became Elton's first British No. 1. Indeed, it became the sound of that particular summer, staying in the top spot for six weeks. His old record company, DJM, would attempt to cash in by reissuing 'Bennie And The Jets,' never before released as a UK A-side. Back in America, Elton reinforced his record-breaking run of live shows by smashing a year-old Rolling Stones house record with seven sellout dates.

Talking of houses, Elton had quit 'Hercules,' his Wokingham home, in early 1976 for 'Woodside,' a mansion in Old Windsor, England, where he would reside into the 1990s. 'I always buy *Country Life* and have a look at houses for sale,' he would later admit. 'But I've got a nice house, a lot of garden and my little recording studio. It's close to London, it's close to the airport and it's close to Watford.' Despite buying a Los Angeles base in the mid-1970s, Elton had always shunned the idea of becoming a tax exile. 'I belong here,' he said simply.

As so often in previous years, in 1976 Elton planned a record release for the Christmas market. *Blue Moves* was his first such release for Rocket Records, but the last to be produced by Gus Dudgeon and with Bernie Taupin's words (entirely, at least). Famous friends chipping in on the backing-vocal front included David Crosby, Graham Nash, Beach Boy Bruce Johnston, and Toni Tennille of the Captain and Tennille.

A double album, *Blue Moves* came clad in a controversial sleeve on which nude men frolicked; indeed, certain critics initially tried to interpret the title as 'Blue Movies.' With regard to the content, parallels with *Goodbye Yellow Brick Road* were obvious. As frequently happens, the first single was the most successful, and 'Sorry Seems To Be The Hardest Word' was indeed a classic. The likes of 'Bite Your Lip (Get Up And Dance)' were hardly in the same class, while 'Cage The Songbird,' a paean to Edith Piaf, begged the inevitable comparison with 'Candle In The Wind.' The general tone of the album was less than optimistic, doubtless due to Bernie Taupin's split with his first wife Maxine. Two of the more cheerful songs were in fact instrumentals, including Elton's 'Theme From A Non-Existent TV Series.'

The reason behind the split with Gus Dudgeon was, reveals the producer, that 'the challenge had gone,' and he gave an insight into Elton's preferred way of working. 'He'd got to the point where he was going into the studio only five days before the album and writing the whole album in those five days – and writing three or four hits. He did it every time – what more could you ask for?'

Two more distinctions came Elton's way in 1977: the

Right: The contemplative musician: Elton performs in November 1977.

Far right: Elton adopts an enigmatic pose for the cover of his 1978 album *A Single Man*. The album contained a hugely successful single: the moving 'Song for Guy.'

first was being honored in Madison Square Garden's Hall of Fame in October, the only rock artist to have received the accolade. But perhaps even more important to Elton was his accession four months earlier to the chairmanship of Watford Football Club. Soccer had been a lifelong passion of Elton's, vying for his attention with those Saturday-morning classes at the Royal Academy (and sometimes winning). But whereas the lad's stocky, less than athletic, physique had prevented him from excelling on the pitch, the piano had offered him a chance of increased stature. Now his success, and its rewards and his public profile, enabled him to buy himself into the game at boardroom level. Indeed, the players would feature on two tracks of his next album as backing vocalists!

But just as soccer players need to pace their game as they get older, and let the ball do the work of the legs, so Elton finally seemed to be cutting back on the punishing work load that had brought him success. He emerged from comparative seclusion to play at a charity gala at Wembley Arena, and it was then that he announced his retirement from live work. He had not actually toured with a band since 1976.

So it was that 1978 was almost a year off; almost, but not quite: the album titled *A Single Man*, released in October, indicated perhaps that Elton was no longer working hand in glove with Bernie Taupin. The sales performance of Elton's first non-Bernie collaboration, 'Ego,' with Gary Osborne, had hardly boded well for the future, reaching just No. 34 in Britain and America in April. As if to retain some link with the past, the album was recorded in Gus Dudgeon's studio, although the producer himself was working elsewhere.

With new wordsmith Osborne (a former jingle writer) under the spotlight, it was ironic that the album's most successful track was an instrumental. 'Song For Guy' was a touching tribute to a messenger boy employed by Rocket Records who had died in a motorbike accident. Reaching No. 4, it was Elton's most successful British single for ages (and his first to utilize a drum machine, though such was the song's plaintive appeal that few noticed or cared). Perhaps its success stirred the performing bug in Elton, for February 1979 saw his first comeback appearance in Sweden, a curtain raiser for a 30-date British tour. However, this would be a tour with a difference: his Anglo-American big band was now history, and Elton had retained only the services of percussionist Ray Cooper.

The dynamic duo played 125 dates in a year, and made history in May 1979 when they opened in Leningrad on the first of eight Russian dates. If one discounts Cooper, Elton John (or 'Alton Yin,' as his name was translated) was the first Western solo pop star to tour there, and his progress was recorded for a TV documentary entitled *To Russia With Elton*. His departure was marked with the release of a second EP of Thom Bell soul sessions. 'Are You Ready For Love' fell in-between the status of a single and an album; treated as the latter by *Billboard*, it reached only No. 51, but No. 42 in the British chart. Normal service was resumed when 'Mama Can't Buy You Love' was extracted as an American single and reached No. 9 in August. One month later, following up the single's success, Elton collapsed on stage at the Universal Amphitheater, suffering from exhaustion due to a bout of flu. Fortunately, after a 10-minute break he had recovered sufficiently to complete the show.

After the sacking of his regular band, his retirement

Far left: Elton pictured with close friend and fellow soccer fanatic Rod Stewart in 1978, the year in which Elton took a well-earned break from his relentlessly hard cycle of work.

Left: The chairman of Watford Football Club proudly leads out his team. Soccer had always been a passion of the English singer, and in him Watford FC found a powerful promoter – if not a player!

Below: Sporting complementary headgear, Elton and 1960s icon Cathy McGowan pose together in 1978.

and the two-man show, it seemed there was little Elton could do to surprise his longtime followers. However, October 1979 saw the release of *Victim Of Love*, an historic album for the main reason that Elton had had a hand in writing precisely *none* of the seven songs he performed. The opening track, 'Johnny B Goode' was, of course, the Chuck Berry classic, but the other half-dozen were the work (with collaborators) of one Pete Bellotte, an associate of Eurodisco producer Giorgio Moroder, who had helped Donna Summer and others to fame. Moroder was absent from the album's listings, which included future Billy Idol producer Keith Forsey on drums, promising young bassist Marcus Miller (who went on to work with Miles Davis), and Toto's Steve Lukather, who contributed lead guitar on two tracks.

What provoked this 'featured vocalist' approach is unclear, but at Nos. 41 and 35 respectively, fans in both Britain and America gave it the thumbs down, the title track only reaching No. 31 stateside. DJM used the opportunity to promote *Lady Samantha*, a rag-bag of

Above: Surrounded by members of the pop group China in 1977, Elton takes a break from rehearsing.

Right: Elton receives an award in 1978 from the *New Musical Express*, the influential British music paper.

Overleaf: In May 1979 Elton, accompanied by brilliant percussionist Ray Cooper, made history by becoming the first Western solo pop star to play a series of dates in the Soviet Union.

early or rare recordings, which at least gave veteran fans the chance to replace a few worn-out singles.

The middle of 1980 saw Elton return to something like form with *21 At 33*, the title indicating the staggering number of albums released compared with his age. Bernie Taupin made a welcome return; now living in Los Angeles with new wife, model Toni Russo, he co-wrote an album with Alice Cooper before recording his own solo album, *He Who Rides The Tiger*, that year. Unknown to many, it was in fact his second effort: he had already released *Taupin* on the DJM label in 1971 (it was titled *Bernie Taupin* in the States).

From *21 At 33* the song 'Two Rooms At The End Of The World' told the tale of two people who were 'mining gold,' while 'White Lady, White Powder' was a no-holds-barred story of cocaine addiction, with the Eagles on backing vocals. Bernie Taupin by no means enjoyed a monopoly on the lyrics front. Gary Osborne

Above: The early 1980s saw a welcome revival of the Taupin-John partnership. Here Bernie and Elton collaborate on the album *Jump Up*, which was written and recorded in the Caribbean.

Right: Elton demonstrates his inimitable sense of humor, performing dressed as Minnie Mouse in 1981. In the same year he bought the scripts of the legendary *Goon Show*.

was still there, but two other choices were interesting: Tom Robinson, a militant Gay Rights figure who had come to fame on the New Wave was one; Judie Tzuke, a pretty, promising singer-songwriter signed to Rocket Records, another. Again, a stellar cast of backing vocalists included Eagle Tim Schmit and, bizarrely, Peter Noone of Herman's Hermits fame. On the musicians' front, Dee Murray and Nigel Olsson rejoined the fold, alongside guitarists Richie Zito, Tim Renwick and keyboard player James Newton Howard.

Hit singles proved hard to come by for Elton in the early 1980s, 'Little Jeannie' at No. 3 in the States being far and away the most successful of the *21 At 33* selection. This did not, however, dissuade Geffen Records from signing Elton for the United States on 21 September 1980. However, 10 weeks later, the assassination of John Lennon would give Elton John cause for thought. 'I Saw Her Standing There,' the live 1974 take that would remain the ex-Beatle's last live performance, was issued in tribute to Lennon, and scraped into the UK Top 40.

1981 would prove a quiet year releasewise, though '*Les Aveux*,' a one-off duet with France Gall that topped the French charts, was one for the collectors. Elton's annual album, and his debut album on Geffen (though he was still on Rocket at home), was *The Fox*. Produced by the Pretenders' studio-Svengali Chris Thomas, a current hot name, the album was a mixture of writers and ideas: the John-Taupin track 'Fascist Faces' (embellished by the Cornerstone Baptist Church Choir) qualified as one of the sillier songs the pair had concocted, while the markedly more sensitive 'Nobody Wins' was a French song rewritten by Gary

Far right: Elton performs in Newcastle upon Tyne, England, in November 1982 at the end of a prolonged world tour which had started in March.

Right: Making a dramatic entrance: a wheelchair-bound Elton arrives in Sydney, Australia in November 1979, having strained his back.

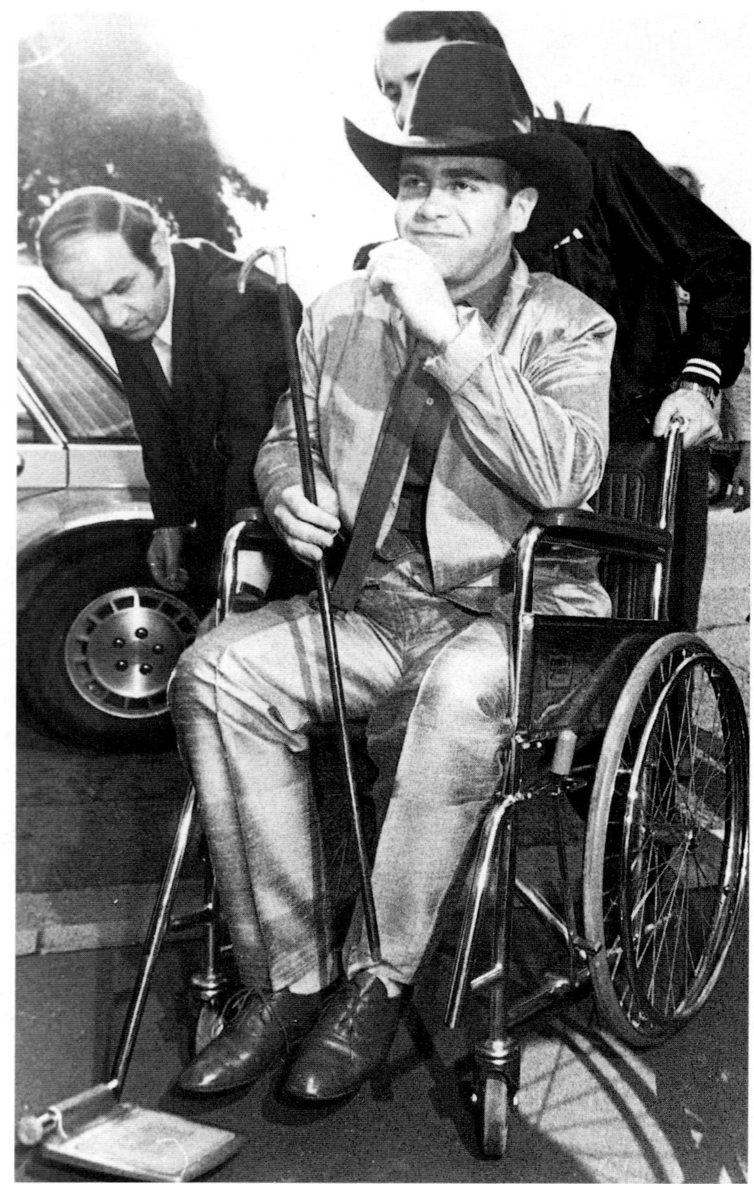

Osborne, and proved the most successful single.

Unusually, the album itself did better in Britain (No. 12) than in the United States (No. 21); so much for the sleeve dedicated to Geffen Records 'for their inspiration (at last).' Further mention must be made of the sleeve: this depicted a room full of wire furniture, along with a stuffed fox. Over the years Elton's album covers had oscillated from the sublime to the ridiculous, but it seemed that his last few had been designed almost to dissuade the casual buyer.

Elton showed his inimitable sense of humor when he bought the scripts of BBC Radio's legendary *Goon Show*. In perfect Goon-speak, he commented: 'I have bought dem because I love dem.' A love of the Goons was something he shared with Prince Charles, and the only concert he played this year also had a royal connection: the 21st birthday of Prince Andrew at a party held at Windsor Castle.

Elton returned to the road for the first time in two years in March 1982 in the unlikely location of New Zealand, with the original Davey/Dee/Nigel band back in harness. A month later the album *Jump Up* was released, which had been recorded on the Caribbean island of Montserrat (Elton had spent much time in the past year on the neighboring island of Antigua). It was a superior collection, with a pair of excellent ballads in the singles 'Blue Eyes' and 'Empty Garden.' Subtitled 'Hey Hey Johnny,' the latter track made public (through Bernie's words) Elton's innermost feelings about the death of close friend John Lennon over two years earlier.

The world tour was destined to move on to Australia and thence to Europe, crossing the United States from June to August. Elton was summoned to the White House to meet President Reagan, also attending the select banquet to honor the Queen's visit to Hollywood, and receiving a pair of coveted ASCAP songwriting awards for 'Chloë' and 'Nobody Wins.' The touring year ended with a record-breaking 14 nights at London's Hammersmith Odeon, marred only when Elton threw a piano stool in a fit of pique and hit a girl in the front row. This unusual display of temper was partly explained by Nigel Olsson's unscheduled absence through illness, but also suggested that the strains of nine months on the road were taking their toll.

It had been a decidedly variable few years in musical terms, so for longtime fans the news that Elton's next album would be written entirely with Bernie Taupin could only be cause for celebration. (Coincidentally, the duo issued a writ against Dick James to claim their back catalogue; this would take fully three years to resolve.) The result of their creative reunion was *Too Low For Zero*, released in a unique and very contemporary die-cut white sleeve, with a colored insert showing through in a graphic effect that represented the title. The album was notable for inspiring Elton's first forays into the medium of the promotional video – then in its infancy – something his showmanship undoubtedly lent itself to. The results were first to become obvious in Britain, where 'I'm Still Standing' smashed its way to No. 4 – eight places better than in the States, land of MTV.

The album had been preceded by the reflective 'I Guess That's Why They Call It The Blues,' with a less than typical (but highly effective) harmonica hook from Stevie Wonder, which made No. 5 in Britain; its American release was delayed until 1984, but then went one place better. Further singles, 'Kiss The Bride' and 'Cold As Christmas' both made the Top 40 in the UK, their quality suggesting that Elton was at something of a creative peak. His personal life too was to reach a turning point, though few could have guessed how, where and with whom.

GRAN
PIANO

These pages: As well as being a master of the keyboard, Elton has perfected the art of the promotional shoot, as can be seen in these alternately serious and wacky poses.

Following pages: Elton can always be relied upon to provide a good show, and although his feet might not always touch the ground, somehow at least one of his hands remains firmly attached to the keyboard. Here Elton is pictured: *top left* in 1978; *top right* in 1980; *main picture*, taking a spectacular tumble in Newcastle upon Tyne, England, in 1982 and; *far right*, preparing to hurl a piano stool, at the same venue.

CHAPTER FOUR
Matters of the Heart

Above: Elton's mother, Sheila Dwight, with his wife Renate at a charity show in December 1984. Mrs Dwight approved of Elton's choice of bride: 'She seems the kind of girl who'll keep Elton in his place.'

Elton's offstage love life had rarely become public knowledge. Unlike many rock stars who traded on their sexuality, his was more of a 'cuddly brother' attraction. The fact that 'Someone Saved My Life Tonight' had related the story of a romance that did not work out suited him down to the ground. However, on Valentine's Day in 1984 Elton amazed the watching world by marrying recording engineer Renate Blauel in an elaborate ceremony at Darling Point, Sydney, Australia. Renate had first met Elton while working as tape operator at AIR Studios in London, where *Too Low For Zero* had been finished. The album bore the dedication 'Special Thanks to Renate Blauel.' Elton's mum was delighted with his choice: 'She's 30, not some slip of a

Right: Elton John and recording engineer Renate Blauel were married on Valentine's Day, 1984, at Darling Point, Sydney, Australia. Sadly the choice of such a romantic date and venue did not prevent the marriage from breaking down.

Below: An emotional moment for Elton, accompanied by Renate, in May 1984 at the start of English soccer's premier fixture, the FA Cup Final. On this occasion Elton's Watford Football Club would lose to Everton.

Right: Elton is passionate about soccer, and for much of the 1970s and 1980s his name was synonymous with Watford Football Club, which blossomed under his patronage. Here Elton poses with the team in May 1983.

girl. She seems the kind of girl who'll keep Elton in his place.' One hundred guests were flown in from England as the groom, resplendent in white tail coat, striped shirt and straw boater, shared the fashion honors with his elegant bride. As for the future, Elton was certain: 'We're not going to be the type of couple who go out to dinner parties and discos – I'm tired of them anyway. We just want to spend some time together. I simply want to be a family man . . .'

Although they were both record-business types, the couple's different lifestyles would obviously entail separations. In April 1984, Elton ran a bath while staying at London's top hotel, the Savoy, and then called his wife in New York. The overflowing water traveled down two floors, causing an expensive amount of damage!

Elton had played many a Wembley date, but few were more emotional than one in May 1984, when he was not the main attraction, but a spectator. Watford

Football Club, which had flourished under his chairmanship and the attention of future England manager Graham Taylor, had reached the FA Cup Final, English soccer's showpiece event. While many might have expected the ebullient Elton to be down on the pitch leading the community singing, for him it was enough to be in the Royal Box, Renate sitting dutifully alongside him. And if the cameras caught him weeping to the traditional hymn 'Abide With Me,' he also had to choke back the tears after his team's opponents Everton confirmed their position as prematch favorites by winning 2-0.

Elton's next single and album shared a heartbreak theme: 'Sad Songs (Say So Much)' and the album *Breaking Hearts* (with a prominent 'Engineered by Renate' credit) reflected the state of his life. Since cutting down on his stateside touring, and following 'gay' revelations, new idols had replaced him in the affections of much of his 1970s' audience, and the album only

reached No. 20 in the States (though sales of the singles were reasonable). He celebrated his first wedding anniversary with the single 'Breaking Hearts (Ain't What It Used To Be).'

Rocket Records by this time existed only to release Elton's own recordings: having by-passed the New Wave and latched on to the short-lived Mod revival with the Lambrettas, Rocket had seen its most promising artist, Judie Tzuke, slip away. This was surprising, since her sensitive singer-songwriter stance had much in common with Elton's work, but, like Kiki Dee, she was to flourish only briefly while under Rocket's wing.

If his label had proved a failure in these terms, Elton found a protégé in whom he was prepared to invest his reputation. George Michael had come to teen stardom in Wham!, a duo whose other half was nonsinging guitarist Andrew Ridgeley which, in truth, was really a vehicle for the once stage-shy singer and songwriter. Although Wham!'s first offerings had been trite anthems directed squarely at the dance floor, it soon became apparent that George Michael, born in Britain of Greek Cypriot parents, was capable of much more. His first solo single, 'Careless Whisper,' released while Wham! still existed, showed he had huge potential, so the logical move was to shed Ridgeley and the backing singers/dancers, who at best had offered moral support, and at worst proved a distraction.

These pages: 1984 proved a busy year for Elton. As well as his marriage, there were performances at the Montreux Pop Festival in May (*above*), and at Wembley Stadium, England in June (*left*).

Overleaf: The special musical relationship between Elton and George Michael has thrived for over a decade. *Left*: the duo pictured at the Live Aid concert in 1985; *right*, Elton and George mark the passing of George's group Wham! in some style in July 1986.

Above: Elton is always ready to offer his services for a good cause. Here he plays at the Prince's Trust concert at Wembley Arena in June 1987.

Right: In August 1984, not long after his marriage, Elton put one of his customized pianos up for sale at the British auction house, Sotheby's.

Far right: Ever prepared to make fun of himself in order to raise money for charity, at a fundraising show in London in December 1984 Elton dressed appropriately to perform 'There Ain't Nothing Like A Dame.'

Far left: In 1985 Elton's role at the Ivor Novello Awards was as a presenter. In 1986 it would be his turn as, along with Bernie Taupin, he received an award in recognition of their outstanding contribution to the British music industry.

Left: Elton leaves the British High Court in June 1985. His legal battle with Dick James Music over royalties would finally be settled in his and Bernie's favor in 1986.

George (real name Georgios Panayiotou) had emulated Elton (a longtime idol) by choosing a snappy name. When Elton presented him with the prestigious Ivor Novello Songwriter of the Year award in March 1985, he was its youngest-ever recipient. The award's presenter was happy to go on record as regarding George as 'a major songwriter in the tradition of Paul McCartney and Barry Gibb.'

The mutual-admiration society continued, and in no little style: Elton guested (in full fancy dress) at Wham!'s concert at Wembley Stadium on 28 June 1985, duetting with George on 'Candle In The Wind.' George repaid the compliment at the same venue two weeks later, contributing the backing vocals to Elton's performance at Live Aid of 'Don't Let The Sun Go Down On Me,' a song they would revive together in 1992. Elton's next album, *Ice On Fire*, saw the youngster provide backing vocals on 'Nikita' and sing a duet with the main man on 'Wrap Her Up,' a song that had more than a touch of Wham! about it. Indeed, their video antics were more suited to teenagers than to someone nearing 40. 'Nikita' was accompanied by an extravagant video, directed by Ken Russell (with whom Elton had worked on *Tommy*), that reflected the song's 'love across the Iron Curtain' theme. For Elton, it was 'a good single but I can't make it work on stage.'

The album had seen a reunion with producer Gus Dudgeon, an event that was sparked by manager John Reid. 'He'd been on at Elton saying maybe it was time to give me a call . . . I was cautious so I said I'd come

Left: Few artists have toured as consistently as Elton John. Here a poignant moment from his performance at Wembley Arena, London, in December 1985.

Below: Festooned with ropes of pearls, Elton prepares to present his young protégé, George Michael, with the Ivor Novello Songwriter of the Year award in March 1985.

over and listen to the songs . . . they were just *fantastic*. How could I say no?' The empathy between the two that still existed perhaps explained the reason why some of the albums released in the nine years that had elapsed since they had last worked together on *Blue Moves* had been less than successful. 'He stayed completely out of the way when he wasn't required,' explained Dudgeon, adding tellingly 'but if he heard something he didn't like, 99 percent of the time he'd know it was something I didn't like either so it would get knocked out.'

Aside from Davey Johnstone and Fred Mandel from his band, Elton let Dudgeon hire other musicians, including John Deacon and Roger Taylor from Queen, and Sister Sledge on backing vocals. One of the tracks, 'Shoot Down The Moon,' was originally written as a James Bond theme; unfortunately Elton had not told the Bond film-makers his plan before sending them a demo tape, and they returned it, having already hired Duran Duran. Dudgeon persuaded Elton to cut it in some spare studio time, and it became a highlight of the album.

The specter of the killer disease AIDS had already made itself felt, mainly in the States, and Elton was happy to lend his name and talents to helping a good cause in the battle to eliminate it. 'I've lost more people to this disease than any other,' he would tell BBC radio. Released in early 1986, the 'charity' record 'That's What Friends Are For' followed Band Aid and USA For Africa in hitting the top of the American chart (and No. 16 in Britain) and thereby raised large sums of money for a worthy purpose. His partners-in-song were Gladys Knight, Stevie Wonder and Dionne Warwick, under whose name the record was released.

January 1986 also saw the final resolution of the dispute with Dick James Music over royalties. On 29

Left: Comedian Billy Connolly and Elton share an uproarious joke at the Ivor Novello Awards ceremony in 1986.

Right: Elton has been a friend of the British royal family since the mid-1970s. In 1981 he performed at Prince Andrew's 21st birthday party at Windsor Castle, and in 1986 he and Renate were guests at the wedding of Prince Andrew and Sarah Ferguson at Westminster Abbey.

Overleaf: Within just eight days in June 1986 Elton guested at two major pop events. *Inset*, Wham!'s farewell concert; *main picture*, the all-star Prince's Trust concert.

January the High Court in London decided in Elton and Bernie's favor, awarding them £5 million in back royalties. James' son Stephen had claimed that if Elton won 'the music business is finished,' but although Judge Nicholls compensated the duo for concealment of royalties, they were not given their copyrights back, and thus failed in their main objective.

With his fabulous wealth, it was doubtful whether the odd few million made any appreciable difference to Elton's bank account, and his willingness to work for charity continued. 20 June 1986 saw him star in the first concert by the Prince's Trust, an organization fronted by the Prince of Wales. Elton shared the limelight with Bryan Adams, Eric Clapton and Tina Turner, before commencing a US tour in Detroit in August. In between times, he and Renate were guests at the wedding of Prince Andrew and Sarah Ferguson, whose friendship, it was said, had helped the Johns come through some rocky times. In November the customary pre-Christmas Elton John album appeared, but 'Leather Jackets' was to prove a commercial trough. In reaching the US No. 91, it was far and away his worst-performing release there, while a No. 24 position in Britain was better, but still disappointing.

In 1985 Elton had charted in Britain with 'Act Of War,' a song originally offered to Tina Turner but which she had turned down. He ended up recording it with Millie Jackson, and a suitably silly video pointed up a good-humored battle of the sexes. The experience of sharing a microphone clearly appealed: the previously mentioned George Michael duet on 'Wrap Her Up' was followed by double acts with Cliff Richard ('Slow Rivers') and Jennifer Rush ('Flames Of Paradise'). Elton would also team up with Aretha Franklin a few years later for 'Through The Storm.'

When he returned to Australia late in 1986 for the first

time since his marriage, the stakes were high for Elton. Commercially, he was at a low point, while the gossip columns were suggesting that his married life was as patchy as his recent hair transplant. However, Elton confronted the critics with a show that saw the most outrageous costumes for ages, and one which spanned the decades. For the first half, he would dress in a Mohican or Tina Turner wig to rock the house, then return as a bewigged, frock-coated Mozart to play, if not classical music, a selection of his own classics that inevitably and deservedly won rapturous applause.

Following this success, a live recording date was set – his first real live album, discounting the contractually-obligated *Here And There* – plus a televised concert, playing to 6 million viewers, Australia's largest-ever TV audience. Yet although he had yet to realize it, Elton was heading for trouble. Throat problems saw him, in Gus Dudgeon's words, 'knee-deep in Kleenexes' on stage. Then, on 9 December, he collapsed in mid-performance in Sydney, an event that attracted world-wide headlines. On 5 January 1987 the cameras were transmitting pictures of the singer in a hospital bed, preparing for throat surgery.

Twelve months' rest and recuperation was the prescription – and that was not the only break in prospect: two months later, the Johns announced their separation. Renate left 'Woodside' for a London flat, though in public Elton claimed the marriage was not over. 'We're known as "The Odd Couple,"' he insisted, 'and that's fair enough. But we still get on very well.'

By April, the voice, if not the marriage, seemed to be on the mend when Elton appeared at an AIDS benefit show in London. His determination to carry on was confirmed when he signed again with Geffen for the States, but their *Greatest Hits Volume Three* only made No. 84 in the American charts. Rather more successful was the double LP *Live In Australia* which, presented as a boxed set, made No. 24 in America (but only No. 70 in Britain). The balance was redressed somewhat when a live performance of 'Candle In The Wind,' recorded with the Melbourne Symphony Orchestra, made the Top 5. The album was later repromoted without its box and reached the UK No. 43 early the following year.

But 1987 would be remembered more than anything else as the year in which *The Sun*, Britain's top-selling tabloid newspaper, set out to crucify Elton John, and failed. 'Elton In Vice Boys Scandal' was the first of several stories which inspired a mind-blowing total of 17 writs from the singer, dated from February to September 1987. By Christmas, Elton had been vindicated, and won not only £1 million in damages, but a groveling front-page apology. 'They can say I'm a fat old sod,

Far left: Australian audiences were wowed in 1986 by Elton's stunning range of stage costumes, including this outrageous wig.

Left and below: Although Elton put a brave face on his harrassment by the British tabloid press (*left*), 1987 was not a good year. He was in ill health and his marriage was in trouble.

they can say I'm an untalented bastard, they can call me a poof, but they mustn't lie about me,' Elton told the *Daily Express*.

However, all did not seem well when Elton tried to sell his controlling interest in Watford FC to Robert Maxwell, but then backed out at the last minute. His instincts were right: the newspaper tycoon later reigned controversially at Oxford and Derby County before drowning in a mysterious accident at sea.

If his uncharacteristic desire to be rid of Watford FC suggested a mid-life crisis, then the release in July 1988 of *Reg Strikes Back* confirmed it. The album's cover was awash with stage regalia, uniforms, spectacles and memorabilia, with the 'real Reg Dwight' stepping out from behind them. While he had stopped short of changing his name back and renouncing Elton entirely, this had clearly been an option under consideration. In early September 2000 items of Elton's memorabilia went under the hammer at Sotheby's auction house in London, including everything from gold disks to spectacles, to his giant 'Pinball Wizard' boots as worn in *Tommy* (which alone fetched $11,000). 'My life and house were cluttered,' Elton explained. 'I never threw anything away, it was all becoming very complicated. So getting rid of everything swept out all the cobwebs. I wanted to start again.'

Far left: Despite recent throat surgery, Elton appeared at an AIDS benefit concert at Wembley Arena in April 1987.

Above: Elton performs with George Harrison and Eric Clapton at the Prince's Trust concert in 1987.

Below: Elton emerges triumphant from court in December 1987 having been vindicated in his stand against *The Sun* newspaper. In addition to a payment of £1 million in damages, he received a front-page apology.

CHAPTER FIVE
I'm Still Standing

Above: Elton has many famous friends. Here he and Renate prepare to fly to New York in the company of Ringo Starr and his wife Barbara Bach, and George Harrison's wife Olivia.

Reg Strikes Back, like *Captain Fantastic* . . . before it, was a point of reappraisal. Renewed success followed: when 'I Don't Wanna Go On With You Like That,' an ungainly-titled stomper, ended up at No. 2 in the States in September 1988, the record blocking its ascent to becoming Elton's first solo US No. 1 since 1975's 'Island Girl' was George Michael's 'Monkey.' Elton concluded an eventful month – even by his own standards – on 23 September, when he played five sell-out nights at Madison Square Garden. The last night, his 26th, beat the Grateful Dead's record – at least it wasn't the Beatles' again! The support act was Wet Wet Wet, the latest beneficiaries of Elton's musical

Right: The late 1980s was not a particularly happy period for Elton, and his choice of clothes often seemed to reflect his despondent mood.

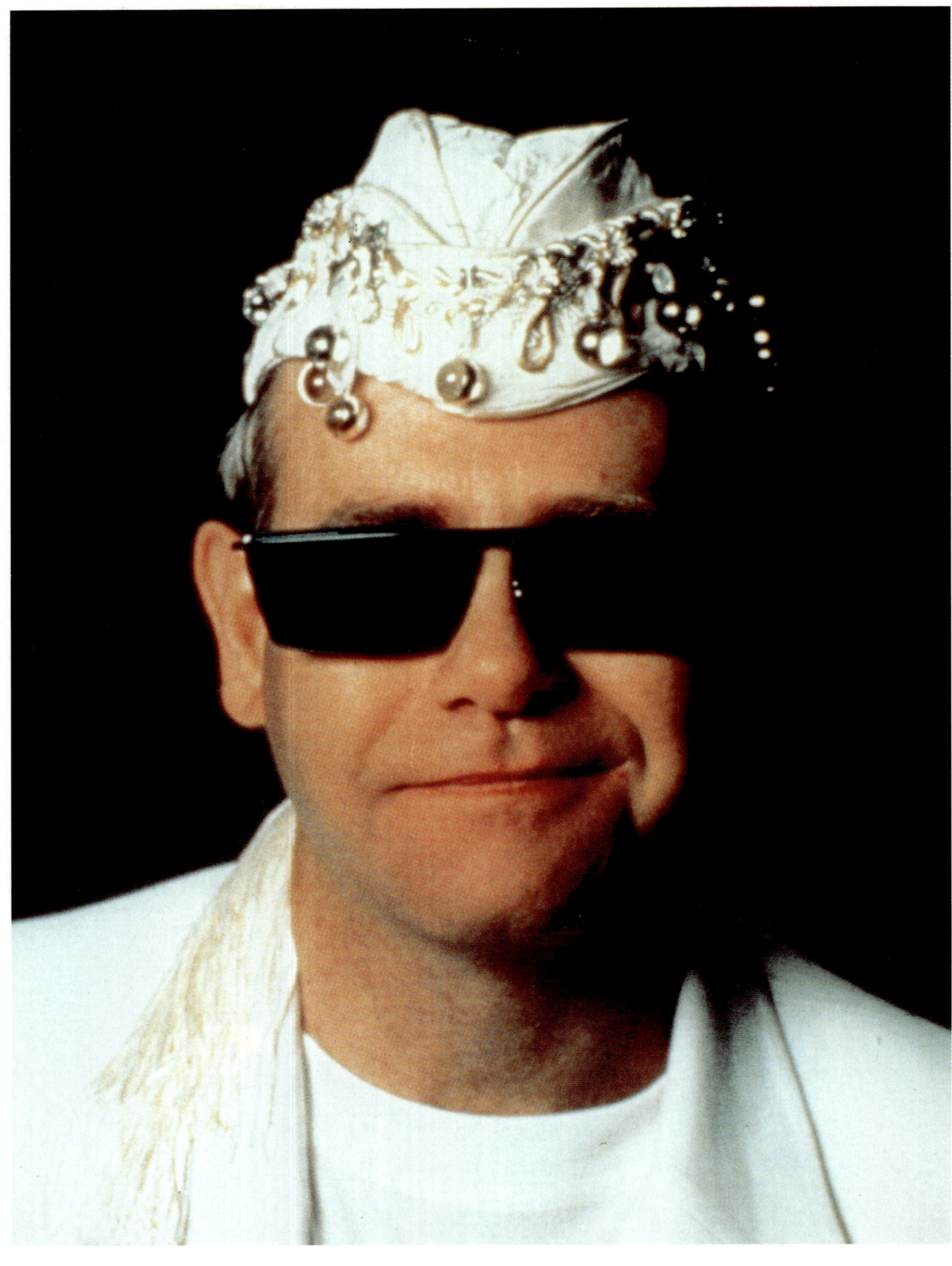

Left: Elton adores fashion and is constantly experimenting with his look. Here he opts for a white ensemble, topped by an elaborately decorated cap.

Right: Elton and Renate attend a charity performance of 'Back With A Vengeance' in London in May 1988. Despite presenting this united front, they would announce their separation only six months later.

patronage; unlike George Michael, however, the group had yet to top the master. Elton stayed in the States to write and produce a single, 'The Rumour,' for Olivia Newton-John, while November 1988 saw the announcement of an 'amicable' divorce from Renate as 'A Word In Spanish' nudged into the US Top 20.

Six nights at Wembley Arena in May 1989 focused on a perennial problem: how to run the gamut of his hits without upsetting too many people. Soul acts habitually contract their finest moments into medleys, but Elton gave full value to 'Burn Down The Mission' as well as to mid-period hits such as 'Philadelphia Freedom' and 'Daniel.' His new look was a baggy purple suit, black T-shirt, porkpie hat and Ray-Ban sunglasses. But worse than that, the grand piano had been supplanted by a digital keyboard – not quite the thing to rest your foot on while rippling through the arpeggios. 'It's not a £300,000 electric organ as you may have read,' Elton explained, adding 'besides, I thought my organ was worth a million quid!' It was not going to be the last reference to *The Sun* saga. 'Thank you for all your support over the last two years: I couldn't have come through it without you,' raised a thunderous cheer. The encore was 'Saturday Night's Alright For Fighting,' performed in a lime-green suit, top hat and Lennon-style glasses – remarkably restrained, all things considered. 'Constant, reliable, an unchanging icon of British pop,' said British newspaper *The Independent*. Few audience members were admitting to being *Sun* readers . . .

The next album was *Sleeping With The Past*, an R & B-flavored album nodding its acknowledgment to 1960s' soul and R & B, and described by Elton as 'the first thing I've done for years without personal problems

clouding my mind. That's probably why it's so up. I'm getting my form back.' With similar reference points to *Don't Shoot Me, I'm Only The Piano Player*, the omens were right for a bestseller, and one track in particular bore these out.

It had long been one of pop's favorite trivia questions: which million-selling singer has never had a solo British No. 1 single? Fourteen years after his Kiki Dee duet, Elton finally made it with 'Sacrifice,' almost inevitably a John-Taupin ballad. The profits from the single were donated to the Terrence Higgins Trust for AIDS research, while its success also helped *Sleeping With The Past* to sales of five million. The decision to align himself with AIDS research with 'Sacrifice' was one taken after Elton had struck up a friendship with teenage hemophiliac Ryan White. When Ryan finally succumbed to the disease, contracted after a blood transfusion, Elton traveled to Indianapolis to act as a pallbearer.

The Very Best Of Elton John swept all before it in the Christmas 1990 album sales' stakes, though it was noticeable that the fertile, if less commercially successful, period between 'Your Song' and 'Rocket Man' had been completely omitted. Perhaps the title 'Greatest Hits' would have been more accurate. A tribute album to Elton and Bernie, fittingly entitled *Two Rooms*, after the *21 At 33* track, was released in late 1991. Great names like Eric Clapton, Kate Bush, The Who, Rod Stewart and, inevitably, George Michael all collaborated on the star-studded cover-version project.

Taupin himself was living quietly in Los Angeles, in the same house he had bought in 1972. Now a US citizen, he had even flown his parents out to join him and his second wife Toni. Professionally, he was dabbling in rock-video direction and writing two US chart-topping singles with British musician Martin Page for other artists: 'We Built This City' for Jefferson Starship, and 'These Dreams' for Heart. There had also

Left: Elton in transit at London's Heathrow airport in January 1990. Even when dressed casually, Elton takes pains to co-ordinate his outfit.

Above left: Elton proudly displays yet another honor – the ASCAP award, presented in October 1991 for his hit single 'Club At The End Of The Street.'

been a third solo album – *Tribe* – released in 1987.

Boxed sets were becoming very popular, and it was of little surprise when Elton's traditional pre-Yuletide offering in 1991 was packaged as a Christmas box. *To Be Continued* offered little that the ardent Eltonophile would not already have in their collection, apart from the demo version of 'Your Song,' written at a time when to sing the line 'don't have much money' required no artistic license whatsoever! The album did battle with boxed sets from Crosby, Stills and Nash, the Carpenters and King Crimson – the band Elton had auditioned for around the time 'Your Song' was written!

Intriguingly, there was a statement of intent in the album's accompanying booklet. 'My old life stops with the release of this history,' it said. 'A new life starts here.' Manager John Reid might have said the same thing, and indeed did in so many words when he went public in 1991 over his battle with alcoholism – a problem Elton himself had also faced. 'I have been

Above: An unusually bashful Elton peeps out from behind the stage curtain at the Palais des Sports, Paris, in March 1989.

Left: For his 1989 tour Elton replaced his customary grand piano with a digital keyboard, which excited much media comment. Here Elton gives it a pounding at the Palais des Sports, Paris.

drinking since I was 15 years old and it's always very tough to accept that you need treatment,' Reid confessed, adding that he had become particularly depressed after a couple of close friends had died of AIDS. One more of these was added to the tragic roll call when Queen singer Freddie Mercury died in November 1991. Elton's 100 pink roses bore a card saying simply 'Thanks for being my friend: I will love you always.'

After John Reid's admission, Elton elaborated on his own drugs, alcohol and bulimia difficulties in a no-holds-barred television interview with David Frost in November 1991. He told Frost that his mother had moved to Spain two years previously with his dearly-loved stepfather Fred (or Derf, as Elton dubbed him) in protest at her son's excessive lifestyle, but had now moved back. A book, Philip Norman's *Elton*, that had described his 'little moments' was 'spot-on,' he ack-

Above: Ever the professional, Elton performs in November 1991. In this month he bravely revealed in a television interview with David Frost that he had battled against huge drug-related and emotional problems: 'In the end, I was emotionally dead. A carcass.'

Below: Elton campaigns tirelessly for AIDS research. Here, along with British comedian Rowan Atkinson, he participates in Hysteria 3, a fundraising revue in London in July 1991.

Right: Elton's decision to donate the profits from his hit single 'Sacrifice' to the Terrence Higgins Trust was prompted by the death of hemophiliac Ryan White. Elton and Elizabeth Taylor, pictured together at a gala dinner for the AIDS Crisis Trust in November 1991, are dedicated fundraisers for the cause.

nowledged. He also paid tribute to Renate whom, it seemed, he had not divorced as had been believed, but did not remain in contact with her at her own request. 'I married a wonderful girl who I thought would change me . . . but I realized I'd made a mistake . . . Nothing changed me because I had a very big problem and I think I made Renate very unhappy.'

From 1976 to 1990, Elton told Frost, he suffered 'periods of intense and utter pain and distress . . . I became angry and disdainful, spiteful and irritable. I was totally selfish and, in the end, I was emotionally dead. A carcass. Just like Elvis Presley before he died.' The catalyst was someone he fell in love with, who 'was trying to tell me something – if I didn't act quickly I was going to die.'

Elton's response was to check into a Chicago hospital where he was treated for alcoholism, cocaine addiction, bulimia and compulsive overeating. On his discharge six weeks later, he had given up alcohol, drugs, white flour and sugar and, just as importantly, had rediscovered his self-esteem. According to reformed alcoholic Beauchamp Colclough, to whose book *Tomorrow I'll Be Different* the singer contributed a foreword, Elton 'craved genuine love and admiration as a person as opposed to shallow hero-worship of his talent . . . Self-recognition is all-important. And he made it.'

Originally released in 1974, 'Don't Let The Sun Go Down On Me' seemed to have become Elton's theme tune for middle age. A remixed version of the track had already been issued in February 1991, presumably to promote the *The Very Best Of Elton John* album, but, more significantly, it had also become part of George Michael's set in his *Cover To Cover* tour that same year. In March, Elton surprised him backstage at a Wembley concert and they spontaneously decided to duet on the song. When Elton came out from the wings the crowd went crazy – an event recreated for the video

that accompanied the single's release in November (although the video was 'faked,' the recording was that of the initial Wembley performance). In February 1992 the track became the seventh stateside chart-topper for both artists (not counting George's Wham! hits), and for Elton it had been a long wait: since 1976's duet with Kiki Dee. It reached No. 1 in Britain, too.

With its elaborate Versace-influenced artwork, *The One* was released in June 1992, and was a suitably successful follow-up to the chart-topping *The Very Best Of Elton John*, reaching No. 2 in Britain and No. 8 in America. Eric Clapton (with whom Elton played a series of high-profile, double-header concerts) guested on guitar for 'Runaway Train,' while 'The One' itself was a trademark ballad that could hardly fail as the lead single – and indeed did not, reaching the UK Top 10.

Released in May 1993, 'Simple Life' broke Elvis Presley's record for the greatest number of consecutive years (23) that an artist had achieved *Billboard* Top 40 status in the singles' market. Yet the sight of a leather-trousered Elton shuffling nervously to a prerecorded backing track in a 'live from Atlanta' link-up on BBC-TV's *Top Of The Pops* (with not a piano in sight) led one to wonder if he had not forgotten what he was good at. The live shows, too, had been a triumph of icing over the musical cake: a shoal of backing singers and supporting players now featured where once a pianist, a nine-foot Steinway and a two-man rhythm section had ruled supreme. But perhaps the fact that the pianist had played on for nearly a quarter of a century after the Troubadour triumph which had started it all was cause for celebration in itself.

Elton's progress on his 1993 world tour was stately indeed and, as befitted his Versace-inspired image, the associated T-shirt was one everyone wanted to be seen in. Even tennis champion Steffi Graf made her way to the tennis courts at Wimbledon in one, cementing the sporting link that began with Billie Jean King and

Far left: Elton revives old memories by appearing as a guest star in The Who's rock opera *Tommy*, performed at the Royal Albert Hall, London, in November 1989.

Left and below: The death of Queen's lead singer, Freddie Mercury (*left*, performing at Live Aid in 1985) from AIDS came as a severe blow. *Below:* A devastated Elton attends Freddie's funeral in November 1991.

Overleaf: The Who staged a special performance of *Tommy* in November 1989 in aid of underprivileged children. Pete Townsend, Elton and Phil Collins (in heavy disguise as Uncle Ernie) clearly thoroughly enjoyed the occasion.

Left: In November 1991 Elton's father, Stanley Dwight, who was divorced from Elton's mother Sheila, made very public his desire to see Elton 'before his death.'

Below: Elton's moving tribute to Freddie Mercury was a heartfelt message, accompanied by 100 pink roses.

Right: 'Don't Let The Sun Go Down On Me' – by May 1992 Elton seemed to have put his problems behind him. Pictured here in concert in Oslo, Elton looks noticeably more happy and healthy than at any time in the preceding five years.

was celebrated in 'Philadelphia Freedom.'

The trade-press advertisements were understandably immodest. 'Twenty-four countries, 150 shows, three-and-a-half million people, sold out – thank you Elton,' chorused manager and promoters alike of the year-long set of dates that had taken the man and his band from Oslo to Istanbul via Europe, North and South America, Australasia and Southeast Asia, then North America and Europe again.

But disaster struck in Israel in mid-June, with what manager John Reid described with appropriate drama as 'the worst experience in Elton's showbusiness

Above: From left to right, Bernie Taupin, Elton and Warner/Chappell Music chairman Les Bider sign a contract worth $39 million in November 1992.

Right: Elton with manager John Reid in May 1988. It was as a result of Reid's public admission of alcoholism in 1991 that Elton came clean over his own struggle with drugs, alcohol and bulimia.

Far right: Elton in the company of a furry friend.

REVLON
REVLON
REVLON
REVLON
REVLON
REVLON
REVLON
REVLON

Far left: Supermodel Claudia Schiffer joins Elton John to promote his Revlon-sponsored 1993 world tour.

Above: In 1991 Elton renewed his association with Watford Football Club by becoming a director. In 1993, however, he resigned the post, due to pressure of work.

Left: The Rocket Man – Elton sets himself a punishing schedule, and is apparently constantly on the move. Here he is snapped passing through London's Heathrow airport in September 1993.

career.' One might have expected the security men to be overzealous in what had often been a venue for violence – but the opposite, it seemed, was the case. Bob Dylan, another visiting rock star, was earlier also perturbed to find himself mixing with fans at Tel Aviv airport, where Elton – seemingly permitted no VIP facilities – had to stand in line to have his passport stamped! 'By the time they arrived at the Hilton,' commented Reid, 'a large number of people, mainly press, had blocked the entrance. Despite pleas for help no action was taken and Elton could not reach his room. Order quickly deteriorated and shouting and pushing ensued. Fearing for his physical safety and that of his fans, Elton returned to his car and back to the airport.'

The sellout show was scrapped as the Rocket Man flew back to London, having been clubbed over the head by a camera in the mêlée. However, the personal intervention of Britain's ambassador to Israel, Andrew Burns, saw Elton return the following day to fulfill the engagement. It was a blot on an otherwise stain-free tour . . . but not, it seemed, an indelible one.

The year was also marked by another lawsuit, this time against Britain's *Daily Mirror* newspaper for printing an unsubstantiated article embellishing reports of Elton's bulimia problem. The result was another victory and substantial damages for Elton. Shortly afterward, Elton released his Christmas album. *Duets* contained an eclectic selection of cover versions, featuring Elton and 15 guest performers – names such as kd lang, Leonard Cohen, Little Richard and Tammy Wynette.

Although remaining a shareholder and honorary vice president, Elton had resigned as a director of Watford Football Club on 11 January 1993. 'Over the last two years Elton's constant touring and recording schedule has been particularly punishing,' Watford director (and longtime music-business friend) Muff Winwood said. 'It will keep him away from the UK for the foreseeable future, but we know he will be on the phone regularly, as eager as ever for results and news.' Three months later came reports that Elton was taking acting lessons in preparation for a starring role in a movie about another songwriting legend, Cole Porter.

He had also thrown himself into the Elton John AIDS Foundation, launched in March 1993 on the first occasion of what was intended to be an annual Oscar-night party in Beverly Hills. The profits from all his singles were now going toward AIDS research, along with the proceeds from his European gigs in mid-1993 (spon-

Left: Despite his resignation from Watford Football Club's board of directors, Elton remains a life president of the club, and is not ashamed to wear his loyalty on his cap.

Above left: In July 1993 Elton put his enormous record collection up for auction. In December that same year, Sotheby's in London sold his fabulous jewelry collection, supposedly in order to allow him to concentrate on his new interests – Gainsborough paintings and Staffordshire pottery.

Above: Elton successfully sued Britain's *Daily Mirror* newspaper in November 1993 for a lurid – and untrue – story connected with his bulimia. He is shown here leaving the High Court in London.

sored by cosmetics manufacturer Revlon).

Under the greasepaint, Elton remains a complex individual who, it seems, needs to continue performing and recording to maintain his own self-regard. Yet, given his well-publicized sexual preferences, songs like *The One*'s 'When A Woman Doesn't Want You' require a certain suspension of belief from all but the most innocent listener. Like an actor, Elton is acting out the part which Bernie Taupin has written for him, to his own musical sound track. 'We're actually very opposite kinds of people,' Taupin confirmed. 'We never analyze why the relationship works. I think if you look at it too closely you end up pulling it apart.'

Yet Elton has retained a solid base of public support, affection and admiration that few, if any, of his surviving early 1970s' contemporaries could hope to rival. For, despite the make-up and glamorous stage wear, he is clearly only flesh and blood underneath. 'Just the other night,' he confessed in 1989, 'I forgot the words to "Candle In The Wind." If I was Rod Stewart I'd have got the crowd to sing along and nobody would notice . . . but I found it embarrassing. At least it lets them see I'm human.' Perhaps that very fallibility is the secret of Elton John's two-and-a-half decades of success.

Page 90: Elton is pictured performing in June 1992 in London for the British National Music Day. On this occasion, and on many others that year, he duetted with Eric Clapton.

Page 91: A suitably-garbed Elton arrives at a party hosted by fashion designer Gianni Versace in May 1992.

DISCOGRAPHY

Record Label	Record Number	Title	Release Date
SINGLES WITH BLUESOLOGY			
Fontana	TF 594	Come Back, Baby/Times Getting Tougher Than Tough	July 1965
Fontana	TF 668	Mr Frantic/Everyday (I Have The Blues)	February 1966
Polydor	56195	Since I Met You Baby/Just A Little Bit	October 1967
SINGLES BY THE BREAD AND BEER BAND			
Decca	F 12891	The Dick Barton Theme (The Devil's Gallop)/ Breakdown Blues	February 1969
SINGLES BY ELTON JOHN			
Philips	BF 1643	I've Been Loving You/Here's To The Next Time	March 1968
Philips	BF 1739	Lady Samantha/All Across the Havens	January 1969
DJM	DJS 205	It's Me That You Need/Just Like Strange Rain	May 1969
DJM	DJS 217	Border Song/Bad Side Of The Moon	March 1970
DJM	DJS 222	Rock And Roll Madonna/Grey Seal	June 1970
DJM	DJS 233	Your Song/Into The Old Man's Shoes	January 1971
DJM	DJS 244	Friends/Honey Roll	April 1971
DJM	DJX 501	Rocket Man (I Think It's Going To Be A Long, Long Time)/Holiday Inn/Goodbye	April 1972
DJM	DJS 269	Honky Cat/It's Me That You Need/Lady Samantha	August 1972
DJM	DJS 271	Crocodile Rock/Elderberry Wine	October 1972
DJM	DJS 275	Daniel/Skyline Pigeon	January 1973
DJM	DJX 502	Saturday Night's Alright For Fighting/Jack Rabbit/Whenever You're Ready (We'll Go Steady Again)	June 1973
DJM	DJS 285	Goodbye Yellow Brick Road/Screw You	September 1973
DJM	DJS 290	Step Into Christmas/Ho! Ho! Ho! (Who'd Be A Turkey At Christmas)	November 1973
DJM	DJS 297	Candle In The Wind/Bennie And The Jets	February 1974
DJM	DJS 302	Don't Let The Sun Go Down On Me/Sick City	May 1974
DJM	DJS 322	The Bitch Is Back/Cold Highway	August 1974
DJM	DJS 340	Lucy In The Sky With Diamonds/One Day At A Time	November 1974
DJM	DJS 354	Philadelphia Freedom/I Saw Her Standing There (A-side credited to the Elton John Band; B-side to the Elton John Band, featuring John Lennon and the Muscle Shoals Horns)	February 1975
DJM	DJS 385	Someone Saved My Life Tonight/House Of Cards	June 1975
DJM	DJS 610	Island Girl/Sugar On The Floor	September 1975
DJM	DJS 629	Grow Some Funk Of Your Own/I Feel Like A Bullet (In The Gun Of Robert Ford)	January 1976
DJM	DJS 652	Pinball Wizard/Harmony	March 1976
Rocket	ROKN 512	Don't Go Breaking My Heart/Snow Queen (Duets with Kiki Dee)	June 1976
DJM	DJS 10705	Bennie And The Jets/Rock And Roll Madonna	September 1976
Rocket	ROKN 517	Sorry Seems To Be The Hardest Word/Shoulder Holster	October 1976
Rocket	ROKN 521	Crazy Water/Chameleon	February 1977
Rocket	ROKN 526	Bite Your Lip (Get Up And Dance)/Chicago	June 1977
Rocket	ROKN 538	Ego/Flintstone Boy	March 1978
Rocket	XPRES 1	Part-Time Love/I Cry At Night	October 1978
Rocket	XPRES 5	Song For Guy/Lovesick	December 1978

Rocket	XPRES 13	Are You Ready For Love (Part 1)/Are You Ready For Love (Part 2)	April 1979
Rocket	XPRES 20	Mama Can't Buy You Love/Strangers	August 1979
Rocket	XPRES 21	Victim Of Love/Strangers	September 1979
Rocket	XPRES 24	Johnny B Goode/Thunder In The Night	November 1979
Rocket	XPRES 32	Little Jeannie/Conquer The Sun	May 1980
Rocket	XPRES 41	Sartorial Eloquence/White Man Danger/Cartier Commercial	August 1980
Rocket	ELTON 1	Dear God/Tactics	November 1980
DJM	DJS 10965	I Saw Her Standing There/Whatever Gets You Thru The Night/Lucy In The Sky With Diamonds (Duets with John Lennon)	March 1981
Rocket	XPRES 54	Nobody Wins/Fools In Fashion	May 1981
Rocket	XPRES 59	Just Like Belgium/Can't Get Over Losing You	July 1981
Geffen	49788	Chloë/Tortured (US-only release)	August 1981
Rocket	XPRES 71	Blue Eyes/Hey Papa Legba	March 1982
Rocket	XPRES 77	Empty Garden (Hey Hey Johnny)/Take Me Down To The Ocean	May 1982
Rocket	XPRES 85	Princess/The Retreat	September 1982
Rocket	XPRES 88	All Quiet On The Western Front/Where Have All The Good Times Gone	November 1982
Rocket	XPRES 91	I Guess That's Why They Call It The Blues/ Choc Ice Goes Mental	April 1983
Rocket	EJS 1	I'm Still Standing/Earn While You Learn	July 1983
Rocket	EJS 2	Kiss The Bride/Dreamboat	October 1983
Rocket	EJS 3	Cold As Christmas/Crystal	November 1983
Rocket	PH 7	Sad Songs (Say So Much)/A Simple Man	May 1984
Rocket	EJS 5	Passengers/Lonely Boy	August 1984
Rocket	EJS 6	Who Wears These Shoes?/Tortured	October 1984
Rocket	EJS 7	Breaking Hearts (Ain't What It Used To Be)/ In Neon	February 1985
Rocket	EJS 8	Act Of War (Part 1)/Act Of War (Part 2)	June 1985
Rocket	EJS 9	Nikita/The Man Who Never Died	October 1985
Rocket	EJS 10	Wrap Her Up (Duet with George Michael)/ Restless (Live)	November 1985
Rocket	EJS 11	Cry To Heaven/Candy By The Pound	February 1986
Rocket	EJS 12	Heartache All Over The World/Highlander	September 1986
Rocket	EJS 13	Slow Rivers/Billy And The Kids	September 1986
CBS	650865 7	Flames of Paradise (Duet with Jennifer Rush)/ Call My Name	June 1987
Rocket	EJS 14	Your Song (Live)/Don't Let The Sun Go Down On Me (Live)	July 1987
Rocket	EJS 15	Candle In The Wind (Live)/Sorry Seems To Be The Hardest Word (Live)	January 1988
Rocket	EJS 16	I Don't Wanna Go On With You Like That/ Rope Around A Fool	May 1988
Rocket	EJS 17	Town Of Plenty/Whipping Boy	August 1988
Rocket	EJS 18	A Word In Spanish/Heavy Traffic	November 1988
Arista	9809	Through The Storm (Duet with Aretha Franklin)/ Come To Me (Aretha Franklin solo)	April 1989
Rocket	EJS 19	Healing Hands/Dancing In The End Zone	August 1989
Rocket	EJS 20	Sacrifice/Love Is A Cannibal	October 1989
Rocket	EJS 22	Sacrifice/Healing Hands	June 1990
Rocket	EJS 23	Club At The End Of The Street/Whispers	August 1990
Rocket	EJS 24	You Gotta Love Someone/Medicine Man	October 1990
Rocket	EJS 25	Easier To Walk Away/I Swear I Heard The Night Talkin	November 1990
Rocket	EJS 26	Don't Let The Sun Go Down On Me/Song For Guy	February 1991
Epic	657646-7	Don't Let The Sun Go Down On Me (Duet with George Michael)	November 1991
Rocket	EJS 28	The One/Suit of Wolves/Fat Boys And Ugly Girls	June 1992
Rocket	EJS 29	Runaway Train/Understanding Woman	July 1992
Rocket	EJS 30	The Last Song/The Man Who Never Died/ Song For Guy	November 1992
Rocket	EJS 31	Simple Life/The Last Song	May 1993

ALBUMS

DJM	DJLPS 403	Empty Sky	June 1969
DJM	DJLPS 406	Elton John	April 1970
DJM	DJLPS 410	Tumbleweed Connection	October 1970
DJM	DJLPS 414	17.11.70	April 1971
Paramount	SPFL 269	Friends	May 1971
DJM	DJLPH 420	Madman Across The Water	October 1971
DJM	DJLPH 423	Honky Château	May 1972
DJM	DJLPH 427	Don't Shoot Me, I'm Only The Piano Player	January 1973
DJM	DJLPO 1001	Goodbye Yellow Brick Road	October 1973
DJM	DJLPH 439	Caribou	June 1974
DJM	DJLPH 442	Elton John's Greatest Hits	November 1974
DJM	DJLPX 1	Captain Fantastic And The Brown Dirt Cowboy	May 1975
DJM	DJLPH 464	Rock Of The Westies	October 1975
DJM	DJLPH 473	Here And There	April 1976
Rocket	ROSP 1	Blue Moves	October 1976
DJM	DJH 20520	Greatest Hits Volume 2	September 1977
Hallmark	SHM 942	London And New York	January 1978
Rocket	TRAIN 1	A Single Man	October 1978
Pickwick	PDA 047	The Elton John Live Collection	January 1979
Rocket	HISPD 125	Victim Of Love	October 1979
DJM	22085	Lady Samantha	February 1980
Rocket	HISPD 126	21 At 33	May 1980
K-Tel	NE 1094	The Very Best Of Elton John	October 1980
Rocket	TRAIN 16	The Fox	May 1981
Hallmark	SHM 3088	The Album	September 1981
DJM	DJLP 1	Greatest Hits Volumes 1 & 2	December 1981
Rocket	HISPD 127	Jump Up	April 1982
TV Records	TVA 3	Love Songs	October 1982
Rocket	HISPD 24	Too Low For Zero	June 1983
Rocket	810 062 2	Superior Sound Of Elton John 1970-1975	April 1983
Rocket	814 085 1	Love Songs: Elton John	February 1984
Premier	CBR 1027	The New Collection	April 1984
Premier	CBR 1036	The New Collection Volume 2	May 1984
Cambra	CR 130	Seasons: The Early Love Songs	May 1984
Rocket	HISPD 25	Breaking Hearts	June 1984
DJM	DJMCD 4	Superior Sound Of Elton John 1970-1975	October 1984
Rocket	HISPD 26	Ice On Fire	November 1985
Rocket	EJLP 1	Leather Jackets	November 1986
Rocket	EJBXL 1	Live In Australia	September 1987
Rocket	EJLP 3	Reg Strikes Back	July 1988
Rocket	8388391	Sleeping With The Past	September 1989
Contour	CN 2102	The Elton John Collection	October 1989
Rocket	8469471	The Very Best Of Elton John	October 1990
Rocket	848 236 2	To Be Continued	November 1991
Pickwick	PWKS 4098P	Love Songs	February 1992
Rocket	5123604	The One	June 1992
Pickwick	PWKS 4126P	Songbook	October 1992
Phonogram	5143052	Rare Masters	January 1993
Rocket	5184782	Duets	November 1993

Left: The star in reflective mood.

INDEX

Acknowledgments

The publisher would like to thank Mike Rose for designing this book; Clare Haworth-Maden for editing it; Suzanne O'Farrell for the picture research; Veronica Price and Nicki Giles for production; and Helen Dawson for compiling the index. The following agencies supplied the pictures:

The Brompton Books Picture Library, pages: 6, 7, 12, 25(top), 27, 31, 42, 43, 64, 69, 70, 85, 94
The Hulton-Deutsch Collection, pages: 1, 4-5, 9(bottom right), 16, 17, 20, 24, 25(bottom), 28, 29, 33(left), 34-35, 36-37, 40, 44(both), 65(top)
The Hulton-Deutsch Collection/Reuters, page: 84(top)
Syndication International Ltd., pages: 2-3, 8, 9(top and bottom left), 10, 11, 13, 14, 15, 18, 19, 21, 22, 23, 30, 32, 33(right), 34, 38, 38-39, 41, 44-45, 45, 46, 48, 48-49, 50-51, 51, 52, 53, 54(both), 55, 56, 57, 58-59, 59, 60, 61, 62-63, 63, 65(bottom), 66, 67(both), 68, 71, 72, 73(both), 74, 75, 76, 76-77, 78, 79(both), 80-81, 82(both), 82-83, 84(bottom), 86, 87(both), 88, 89(both), 90, 91
Syndication International Ltd./© Sydney Morning Herald, page: 47
UPI/Bettmann Newsphotos, page: 26